SOURCEBOOK FOR
AUSTRALIAN CROSS-STITCH

SOURCEBOOK FOR AUSTRALIAN CROSS-STITCH

Vivienne Garforth

Kangaroo Press

Acknowledgments

I would like to extend my thanks and appreciation to the following people and companies for their valuable help and encouragement during the compiling of this collection of Australian cross-stitch designs:

Bruce and Rolf Harris for granting me permission to dedicate the book to the memory of their mother Marge Harris.

DMC Needlecraft Pty Ltd for supplying all of the stranded cottons, flower threads and fabrics used in the projects.

My friend Jilna Hatton for obligingly spending many hours helping me to cross-stitch the many different designs.

David Marsh from Crafted Software for patiently answering my questions on working the cross-stitch graphs on my computer and for his help in converting them into a suitable medium for publishing.

Louise Howland from Rajmahal Art Silk threads for supplying me with the full range of coloured silks and Eileen Lang, the Western Australian distributor, for all her help and encouragement.

David and Gail Ireland from Ireland Needlecraft Pty Ltd for their helpful advice on the use of Kreinik metallic threads and for supplying me with blending filaments, braids, cords and ribbons.

Lindsay Muskett for his charming photography, his professionalism and his interest.

Jennifer Newman from Minnamurra Threads for her interest and cooperation and for supplying me with samples of her hand-dyed fabric and stranded cottons.

Julie Hanks from Gumnut Yarns for supplying me with samples of her beautiful hand-dyed silk threads and wools.

Merrilyn and Julie from The Tearose Cottage in Guildford, Western Australia, and Gail McLoughlin from Porcelain & Lace in Midvale, Western Australia, for their generous loans of props for the photographs.

Finally, my thanks go to my long-suffering family for once again living among the general chaos of thread ends, fabric pieces and the horror of unaccounted-for lost needles.

Frontispiece: *The same wattle wreath design (page 60) worked onto three different fabrics for very different results.*

© Vivienne Garforth 1996

First published in 1996 by Kangaroo Press Pty Limited
3 Whitehall Road Kenthurst NSW 2156 Australia
PO Box 6125 Dural Delivery Centre NSW 2158
Printed in Hong Kong through Colorcraft Ltd

ISBN 0 86417 772 0

CONTENTS

Acknowledgments 4
Dedication 6
Preface 8
Introduction to cross-stitch 8
Working the stitches 14
Waste canvas 17
Perforated paper 18
Silk and rayon threads 19
Flower threads with linen 20
Beaded cross-stitch 21
Variegated threads 22
Metallic threads 23
Silk gauze 25
Borders and monograms 26
Painted backgrounds 28
Care and laundering 29
Preparing work for framing 30

DESIGN PORTFOLIO 31
Platypus 32
Numbat 34
Pink heath 36
Small kookaburra 36
Black swan 38
Red-breasted robin 40
Shells 42
Native berries 44
Native orchids 46
Seahorse 48
Red gum blossom 50

Barrier Reef fishes 52
Bauera daisies 53
Lyrebird 56
Dragonfly 57
Wattle wreath 60
Butterfly cloth 62
Baby penguins 66
Butterfly border 68
Sturt's desert pea 68
Grass trees 70
Murray River willow 72
Frill-necked lizard 74
Waratah 76
Echidna 77
Yellow-breasted robins 80
Penguin on a rock 82
Pink fairy basslets 84
Large kookaburra 86
Ulysses butterfly 88
Marsupial mice 90
New Holland honeyeater 92
1920s cottage 94
Dolphins 96
Splendid blue wrens 98
Mottlecah 100
Lemon flowering gum 100
Eastern rosella 103

Suppliers 109
Index 110

Marge Harris, by Rolf Harris

Dedicated to
Agnes Margaret (Marge) Harris

This book is dedicated to the memory of a wonderful lady who passed away on 5 July 1994 at the grand age of ninety-seven.

I first met Mrs Harris when I was only ten years old. My family owned a launch which was moored at the jetty down at the bottom of the Harris's garden on the Swan River in Western Australia. As messing about in boats never really appealed to me, I was fortunate enough to spend many of my precious school holiday hours in her company. We became good friends in spite of the fifty-year age difference and remained so until I was sixteen and began my first full-time job.

Coming from a practical working class background, I was always regarded as the dreamer of the family. Even as a child, when not sewing or embroidering I was reading or writing poems and stories. Mrs Harris encouraged my creativity by listening patiently to my prose, adding a positive comment when required and declaring that when I grew up, I would either write books or work in the theatre and design all the costumes. My mother had hysterics when I told her this and wished fervently that Marge Harris would not fill my young head with such silly nonsense.

I am so grateful now for the influence which this lovely lady had over my formative years with her gentle nature and simple philosophies on life. She saw beauty all around her, whether in her home beneath the tall gumtrees on the banks of the river or in the rugged outback where she loved to fossick for gemstones with her husband Crom. She was one of those very special people who lived life to the fullest, enjoying everything, from a quiet moment reading to participating in amateur theatricals, yet always finding the time and opportunity to offer a kindly word of encouragement or give a pleasant smile of approval to others.

Her remarkable attitude inspired those who knew her to strive for and achieve seemingly impossible goals and I am sure that there are many people in this world, apart from her own family and myself, whose lives are better for having known Marge Harris. She will never be forgotten.

PREFACE

While Australian cross-stitch books are now plentiful, with attractive designs covering all aspects of flora, fauna and social history, most are intended to be copied faithfully. A sourcebook differs from the usual format in that the individual patterns are designed to be enlarged or decreased in size according to the fabric used, and the cross-stitch itself can be worked in alternative threads such as metallics, silks, fine braids and over-dyed threads. The embroidery may be embellished with beads, feathers, shells or other types of collage material.

The method for calculating the fabric required for an individual project is clearly described, so that a motif can be easily adapted for use on a woollen jumper over waste canvas, for inclusion on a miniature box-lid on silk gauze or worked in the traditional method on counted cross-stitch fabric. Small items such as pincushions, greeting cards and needlecases make excellent gifts and fete-sellers and provide easy projects for the novice embroiderer, while a beaded motif on a hand-painted backing fabric is a little more complex and challenging.

I hope that this book of source material for Australian cross-stitch proves to be both encouraging for beginners and satisfying for those who have mastered traditional cross-stitch. Experiment with various methods of fabric painting, beading, collage and framing while creating a project which is totally unique and original, yet still retains the age-old method of cross-stitching over evenly woven threads. The main aim of these designs and instructions is for you to relax, use the various threads and materials which are now available and have a lot of fun!

Vivienne Garforth

INTRODUCTION TO CROSS-STITCH

Cross-stitch has been a traditional method of embellishing costumes for many hundreds of years. It decorates various types of apparel found at ancient sites in Africa, Asia and Europe, worked on fabrics ranging from silk to coarse homespun linen. These days it is used on household linen, folk costumes, casual clothing, framed pictures and church embroidery.

Fabrics

Cross-stitch was traditionally worked on evenly woven linen, but today's cotton embroidery fabrics such as Aida and Linda have been especially created with squares incorporated into the weave. Each square has a small hole in each of the four corners to accommodate the needle and thread.

Aida cloth is woven in four sizes and is measured by the number of woven squares per 2.5 cm (1") of fabric, at 11 holes, 14 holes, 16 holes and 18 holes per 2.5 cm (1").

Linen is woven in various thicknesses of single threads and each cross-stitch is sewn over two threads at a time. For instance, a design requiring 25 stitches will be sewn over 50 threads.

Usually the fabric is counted in inches and pattern books refer to the appropriate number of holes per inch of fabric. To allow sufficient material to complete a certain project, you will need to know the metric calculations.

Cross-stitch on linen is generally worked over two threads so, before calculating the amount of material required, find the number of actual cross-stitches in the design itself and multiply them by two. Belfast linen with 25 HPI equals 98.4 holes per 10 cm or 9.8 holes per centimetre. Irish linen with 32 HPI equals 126 holes per 10 cm or 12.6 holes per centimetre.

Metric equivalents for evenly woven fabrics

Aida 11 HPI equals 43 holes per 10 cm or
   4.3 holes per centimetre
Aida 14 HPI equals 55 holes per 10 cm or
   5.5 holes per centimetre
Aida 16 HPI equals 63 holes per 10 cm or
   6.3 holes per centimetre
Aida 18 HPI equals 70 holes per 10 cm or
   7 holes per centimetre

Hardanger fabric has 22 HPI which equals 86 HPI or 8.6 holes per centimetre; however, on this cloth a cross-stitch is usually worked over two squares of fabric, making it equivalent to 11 HPI fabric.

Calculating the amount of fabric required

1. Count the number of squares in the design both vertically and horizontally—the example is 72 stitches high and 158 stitches wide, with the background fabric being 14 count Aida cloth. Divide these numbers by 5.5, which is the number of fabric holes in each centimetre, bringing the total to 13 cm high x 29 cm wide. (The imperial measurement will be 5" x 11".)

2. Add at least 5 cm (2") on all four sides of the design for clearance, taking the fabric to 23 cm x 39 cm (9" x 15½").

3. Add a turning allowance of 5 cm (2") minimum on all four sides to fold over the edge of the backing board, making the total amount of fabric required 33 cm high x 49 cm wide (13" x 19½").

INTRODUCTION TO CROSS-STITCH

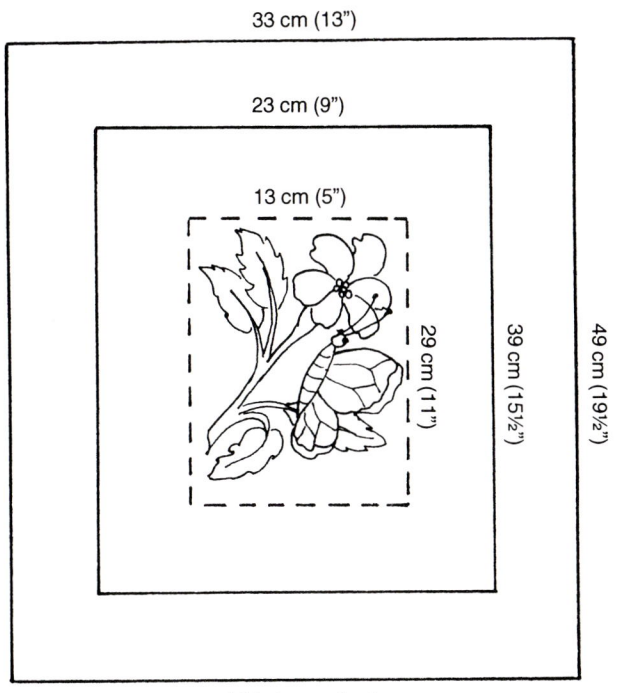

Calculating amount of fabric required

Needles

The needles used in cross-stitch require a long eye and a blunt point so that the threads of the linen or Aida fabrics are not split as the needle travels through the corners of each square. Tapestry needles in sizes 20 and 22 are suitable for coarse material, while sizes 24 and 26 are better for finer linens and smaller woven squares.

Thread and fabric guide

Aida 11 HPI:
   3 or 4 strands cotton or silk
   3 strands DMC rayon
   4 strands Rajmahal rayon

Aida 14 HPI:
   2 or 3 strands cotton or silk
   2 strands DMC rayon
   3 strands Rajmahal art silk
   2 strands Kreinik blending filament with 1 strand cotton or art silk

Aida 16 HPI:
   1 or 2 strands cotton or silk
   1 strand DMC rayon
   2 strands Rajmahal art silk
   2 strands Kreinik blending filament with 1 strand art silk

Aida 18 HPI:
   1 or 2 strands cotton or silk
   1 strand Rajmahal art silk
   1 strand Kreinik blending filament with 1 strand art silk

Hardanger 22 HPI:
 Stitch over two threads and treat as 11 count Aida fabric.

Linen 25 HPI and 32 HPI:
Always work over two threads of weave.
   2 strands cotton or silk
   1 strand flower thread
   1 strand DMC rayon
   2 strands Rajmahal art silk
   1 strand art silk and 2 strands blending filament

LEFT: *Same design of gumleaves cross-stitched onto different types of fabric. Top row: 11 HPI Aida cloth and 14 HPI Aida cloth; second row: 16 HPI Aida cloth and 18 HPI Aida cloth; third row: 22 HPI Hardanger fabric and 28 threads per inch linen with the design worked over two threads*

9

When the stitching has been completed and the end of the thread has been taken through to the back of the work, change to a sharp-pointed needle to weave the excess thread into the back of the cross-stitch before cutting off the remainder. A blunt needle in this situation will catch and drag the stitches.

Threads

There are several varieties of embroidery thread which are suitable for cross-stitch, the best-known being six-stranded cotton which can be divided into smaller numbers of strands. Rayon and silk threads are also packaged in skeins of six strands, while flower threads, which are most suitable for use with linen, are presented in single thread skeins. Threads such as Kreinik metallic blending filaments and braids are already wound onto spools for convenience.

Threads which are sold in skeins should be wound onto cardboard or plastic floss-cards and stored in boxes. This method of storage is particularly useful because the threads can be easily selected by both colour and number. Silk and rayon threads tend to unravel and tangle if not wound onto cards before use.

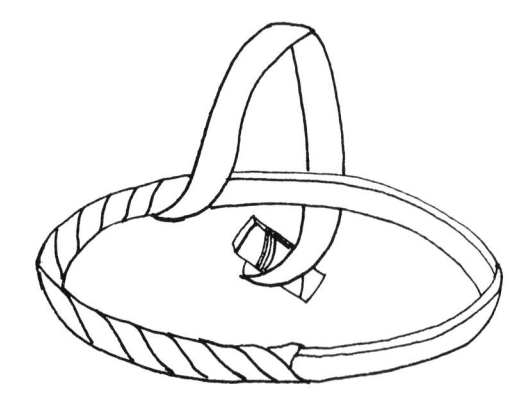

Binding the inner wooden hoop with bias binding

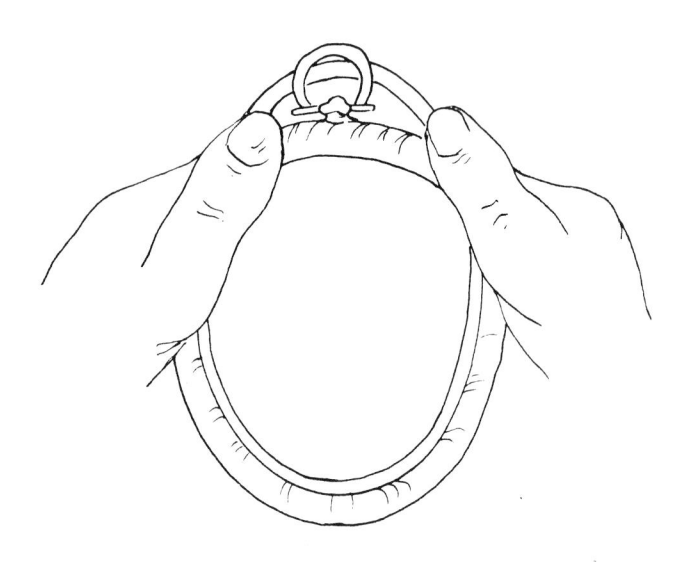

Stretching the flexi-hoop over the rigid inner ring

Embroidery hoops

Cross-stitch embroidery is reliant upon the tension of the individual stitches being totally even, which is easier to maintain if the fabric is held taut in a hoop. There are three main types of embroidery hoops.

Wooden hoops
Traditional hoops used in embroidery, ranging in diameter from 10 cm (4") to 36 cm (14"). Larger sizes are available, but these are intended more for quilting. Each hoop consists of two separate wooden rings, an inner ring in a single piece, and an outer ring cut and joined with an adjustable metal clamp. With this particular type of hoop the fabric will eventually work loose during the sewing process, so it is advisable to bind the inner ring with cotton bias binding or bandaging gauze to provide a better grip. Once the binding is completed, fasten the ends with a few small slip stitches. While this preparation may seem time-consuming and unnecessary it will prove itself worthwhile in the long run.

Flexible hoops
Flexi-hoops, also known as stitch-and-frame hoops, are intended to be used initially as a working hoop. The finished cross-stitched motif is left in the Flexi-hoop, which then becomes the frame.

These frames consist of a rigid plastic inner shape (either circular, oval or square) over which the fabric is placed. A flexible plastic ring stretched over the inner shape holds the fabric extremely taut during the embroidery process. The correct method of stretching the flexible ring over the rigid one is to work from the bottom after having positioned the small metal loop at the centre top. Slowly and firmly 'roll' the flexible ring over the rigid edge of the inner shape with the thumbs until the outer ring slips over the edge at the top and fits snugly against the fabric.

Another form of flexible hoop has a rigid plastic outer ring and a flexible metal inner ring which has two handles at the top. In this case, the rigid ring is laid on a flat surface, the fabric is placed over it and the two metal handles are pressed together to make the inner ring smaller until it is in the correct position. When the handles are released, the metal ring expands to fit tightly into the rigid plastic one, holding the fabric taut.

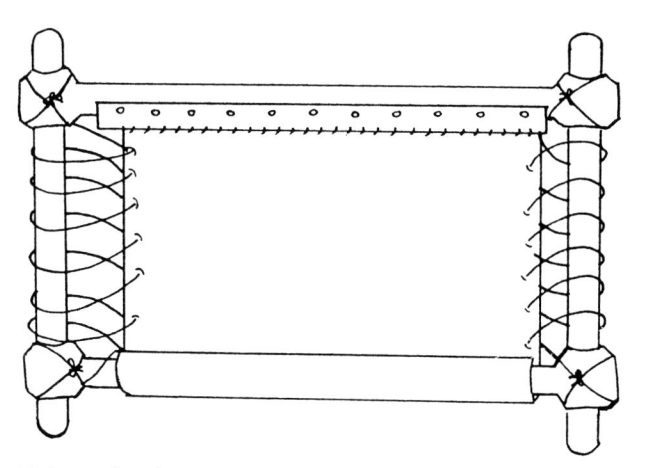

Using a slate frame

Slate frames

A slate frame is used when the area to be cross-stitched is a large one. It is not desirable for a smaller hoop to be moved around over the surface of the material, as it tends to flatten previously worked stitches.

The frame consists of two wooden end pieces and two dowelling rollers which have a strip of webbing stapled along the length of each. The material is sewn to the webbing on each of the two dowels, which are adjusted in the end supports until the fabric is taut. The corners of the frame are held in place and tightened with small bolts and wing nuts. The ends of the fabric are then laced to the end pieces so the fabric is kept taut in both directions.

This method of keeping the fabric taut involves rolling the excess material onto one of the dowels until the cross-stitching has been completed on the exposed surface. Then the lacing at the ends of the frame is unpicked, the embroidered fabric rolled onto the second dowel until the next section to be worked is exposed, the frame tightened and the lacing redone. Using a slate frame like this for a larger embroidery means that completed work is not damaged or flattened in any way.

Preparing the fabric

Before beginning the actual embroidery, certain preparatory steps must be carefully made to ensure the finished project will be worthy of all the hours of pleasurable stitching you anticipate.

Firstly, the edges of the fabric must be either overlocked or zig-zagged by machine, or bound with masking tape, so that they do not fray while the work is in progress. Any marks or fold lines in the material must be removed by hand-washing the fabric with warm water and a mild soap, then ironing the dry fabric with a moderately hot iron.

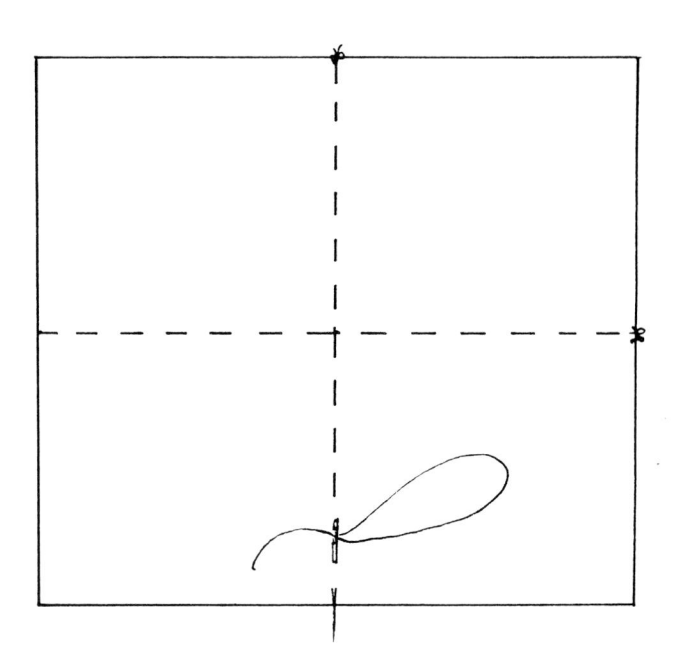

Finding the centre point of the fabric

The centre point of the fabric must be marked, as this is generally the point from which the cross-stitching is commenced. To find this point, run lines of tacking stitches both vertically and horizontally across the middle of the fabric. As most cross-stitch designs are printed on graph paper which is divided into 5 squares per centimetre, size the tacking stitches to each cover 5 threads of fabric. The point where the two tacking lines cross one another is the centre. Do not use a deep colour such as red, black or navy blue for the tacking thread, as these dyes can sometimes leave tiny dots across the material once the threads have been removed. Use a coloured thread which is preferably lighter than the background fabric.

Positioning corner motifs

When working cross-stitched motifs in the corners of a tablecloth or traycloth, mark each corner with tacking stitches to determine the correct position. Once again using stitches which cover 5 threads of the fabric, find the centre point first, then tack around the hem line.

Count the number of stitches across each motif both vertically and horizontally and mark these lines with tacking stitches, commencing at the hem line.

When the motifs mirror-image one another, count across the motif on the shorter side and run the tacking line from one side of the cloth to the other (inside the hem line). Repeat across to the opposite edge. Count

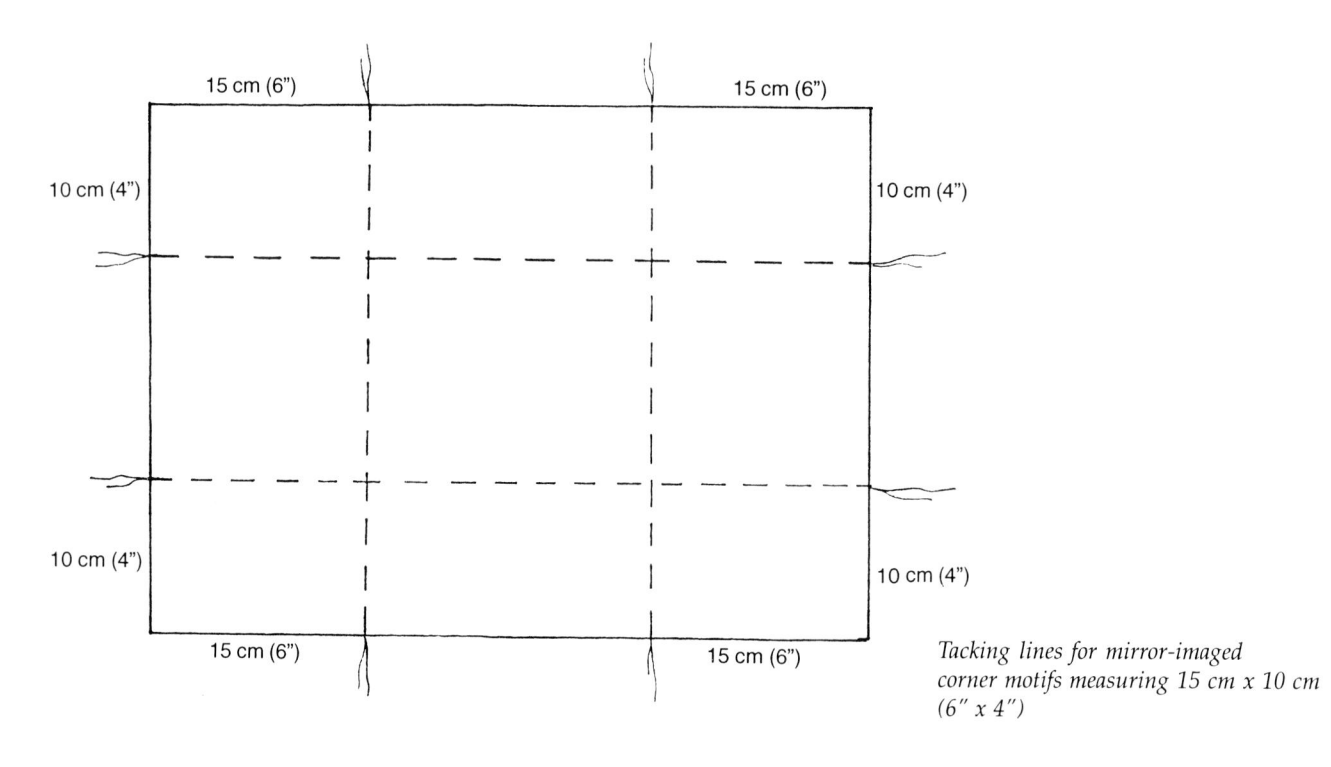

Tacking lines for mirror-imaged corner motifs measuring 15 cm x 10 cm (6" x 4")

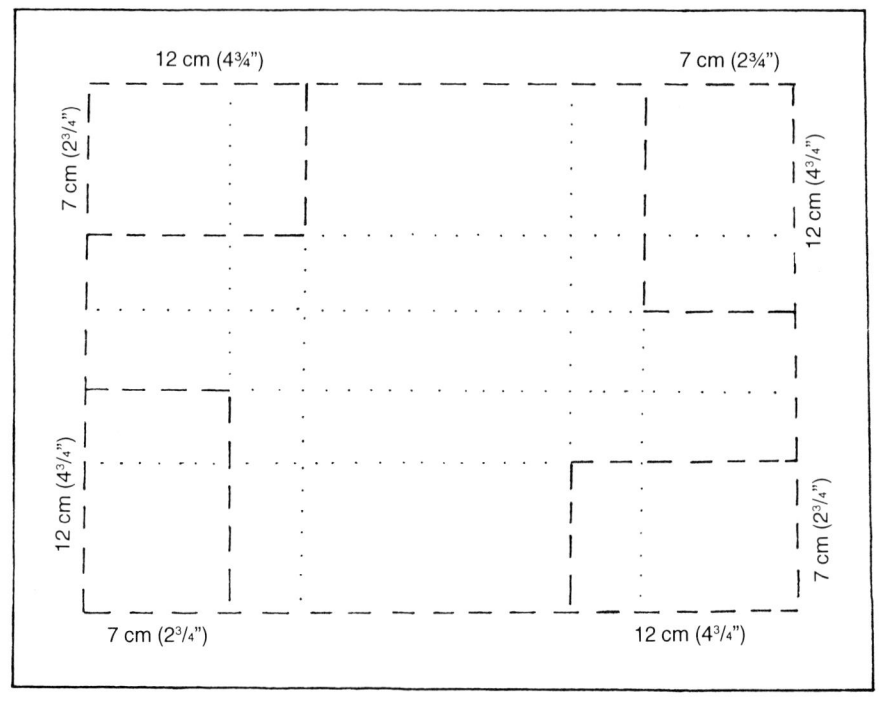

Tacking lines to position corner motifs which all lie in the same direction

across the motif on the longer side and once again run the tacking thread across the fabric to the other side. Repeat across the opposite edge, working from the hem line.

In this way all four corners will be correctly positioned before the embroidery is begun, eliminating tedious counting and recounting of squares later.

Reading the graph

A cross-stitch chart is a grid upon which the design has been drawn in a series of symbols. Each symbol represents a different coloured thread. The key to the symbols and the matching colours is given to the side or below the chart. By following the key exactly you will be

INTRODUCTION TO CROSS-STITCH

able to reproduce the cross-stitched motif onto the evenly woven fabric background.

The vertical and horizontal centre lines of the graph are usually marked by arrows, and the centre is generally indicated with an arrow head or the letter C. Note that where there is an even number of the stitches across the design the arrow falls *on top of* a grid line, making an even number of stitches on either side of that central grid line; where there is an odd number of stitches, the arrow is marked *between* two grid lines, pointing to a row of squares. This row of cross-stitches is the centre row with an even number of stitches worked on either side of it.

Each square on the grid which contains a symbol represents a separate cross-stitch. If a solid dot on the key to the graph is marked 'DMC 310 black', then every square on the graph which is marked with the same solid dot must be cross-stitched on the corresponding fabric square with black thread (DMC number 310). Sometimes part of the design is also marked with a heavy outline, which means that this area of stitching is to be outlined with backstitch once the cross-stitching is completed.

Hints on reading graphs

Occasionally a graph may be too small to distinguish the symbols clearly. One solution to this problem is to enlarge the graph on a photocopying machine and then shade in the different areas with appropriately coloured pencils.

Another problem is 'getting lost' in a maze of complicated symbols so that you are forever counting squares to find the correct position for the stitching. Keep a fluorescent highlighter pen handy and mark off the squares on the graph as they are stitched onto the fabric. The coloured ink is easy to see and yet is quite transparent so that the printed symbol beneath is clearly shown.

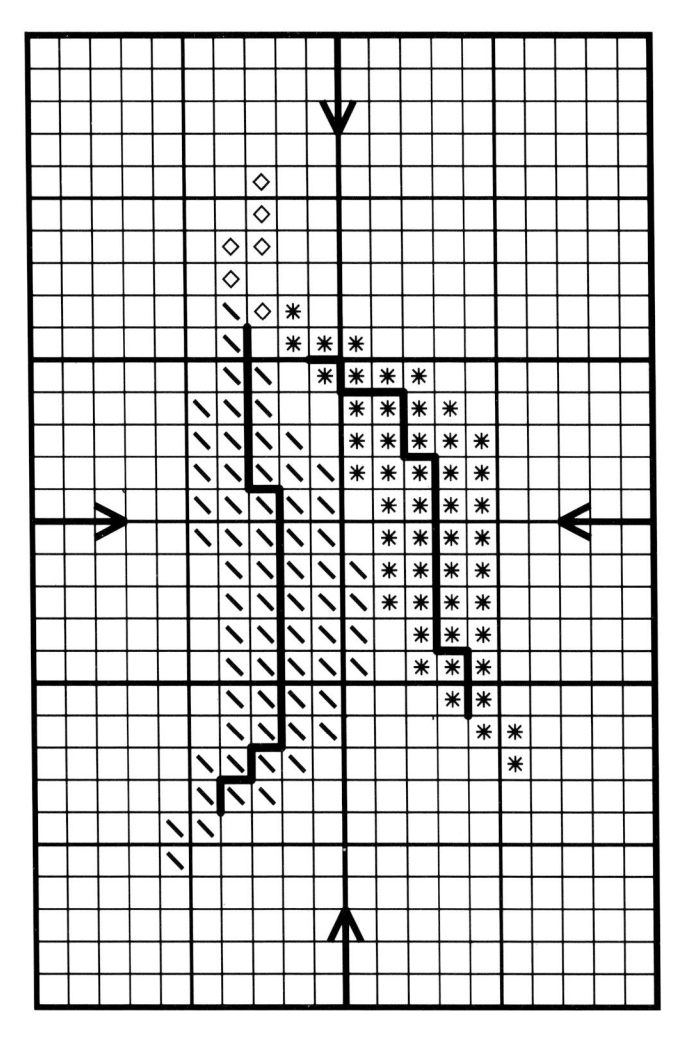

Key

DMC Stranded Cotton

* 319 Very Dark Green
\ 503 Light Green
◇ 869 Brown
⌐ 920 Rust straight stitch leaf veins

Typical cross-stitch graph and key. This is the graph used for the embroidery on page 9, demonstrating the results when the same design is worked in different fabrics and threads

WORKING THE STITCHES

The first thing to learn about cross-stitching is that all the stitches *must lie in the same direction*. While there is no right or wrong way to position the crosses, it is generally accepted that the first or bottom stitch of the cross-stitch is worked from left to right and the second or top stitch is worked from right to left.

Beginning the stitching

There are two accepted ways to begin cross-stitch embroidery and neither of them involves tying a knot at the end of the thread. In fact, knots are a big No-No! in cross-stitch because finished work needs to be as flat as possible, whatever you are doing with it. Knots create little bumps on the right side of the work when it has been pressed smooth in preparation for framing.

When sewing with two strands of cotton or silk, cut a single length of thread twice as long as required. Double the thread over and thread the two cut ends through the eye of the needle. To begin stitching, bring the needle up at the bottom left corner of the cross-stitch and take it down through the fabric at the top right corner, making sure that the needle passes through the loop of thread at the back of the fabric. Once the thread has been pulled taut, the loop will hold the thread securely without an untidy tail.

When sewing with a single thread or with three strands of cotton, cut the thread to the desired length and separate all the strands. Place three strands together again and thread the ends through the needle. Begin stitching by bringing the needle up through the fabric at the bottom left-hand corner of the cross-stitch, leaving a 2.5 cm (1") tail of thread at the back. Take the needle back down at the top right-hand corner of the stitch; as subsequent stitches are worked, catch the tail with the first half of each stitch.

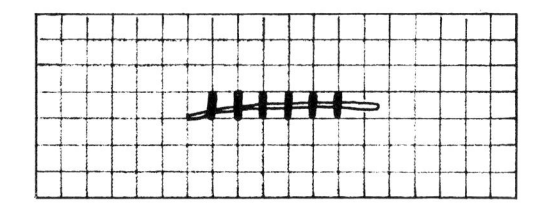

Stitching with the tail caught at the back using an odd number of threads

When working a horizontal row of cross-stitches, work all the left-hand (bottom) stitches first, then return along the row working the upper stitches over the top (working from right to left), as illustrated on the next page.

When working a row of vertical cross-stitches, start at the top of the row. Sew the first half of the first stitch from the bottom left to the top right, then bring the needle up through the fabric at the bottom right-hand corner and down at the top left. Bring the needle out at the bottom left-hand corner of the next stitch down from the one just finished and work another complete cross-stitch.

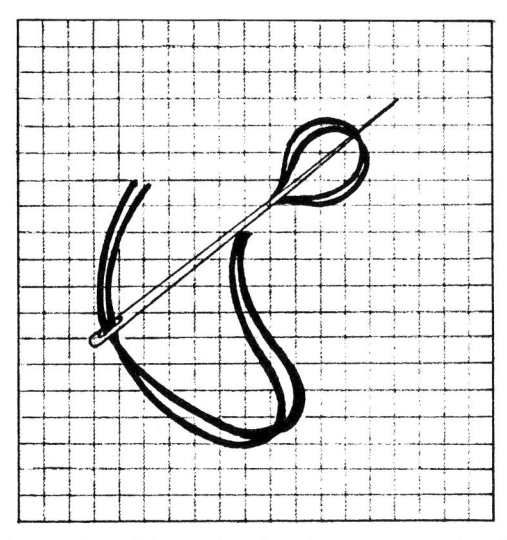

Beginning sewing with two threads using the loop method (back of work)

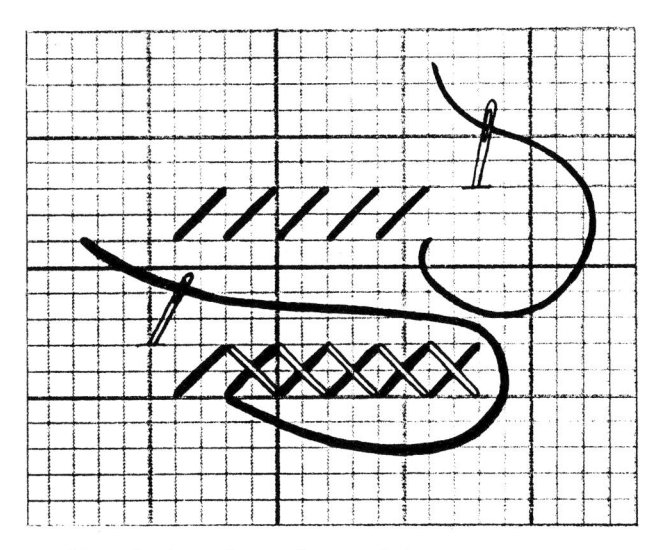

WORKING THE STITCHES

Working a horizontal row of cross-stitches

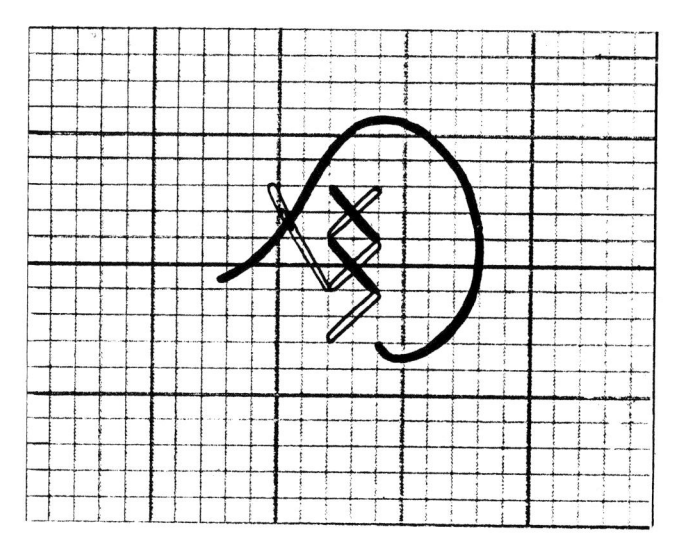

Working vertical rows of cross-stitch

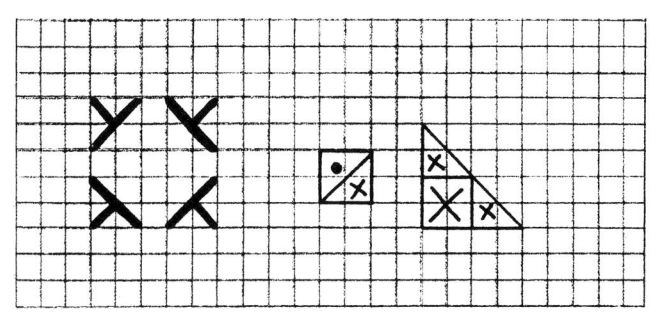

Working with half crosses

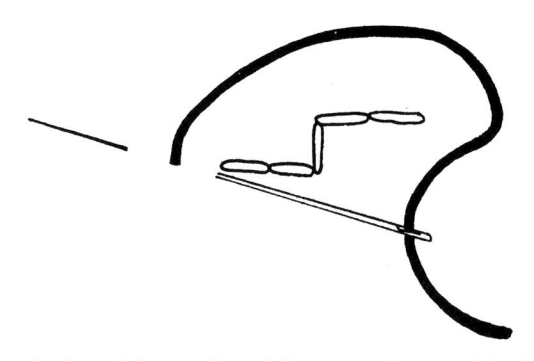

Working backstitch from right to left or top to bottom of the line of stitches

Using half crosses

Sometimes a design will call for a diagonal edge to be formed, either between two colours on the one square of fabric or along the outside edge of the pattern. On these occasions we use a half cross, which can be sewn in all four directions. Half crosses are usually shown on a graph by a solid line drawn diagonally across a square with a colour symbol on either side of the line, as shown in the diagram.

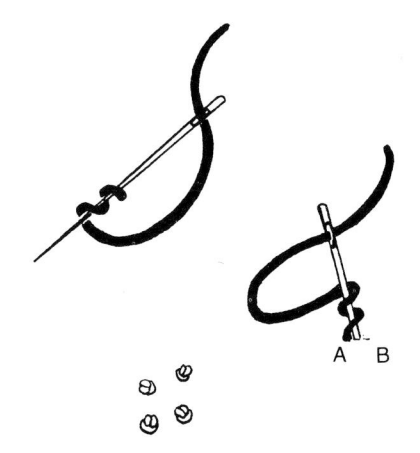

Complementary stitches

The three other stitches most often used in conjunction with cross-stitch are backstitch, French knots and straight stitch.

Backstitch
Backstitch is used mainly to outline areas of cross-stitch and is worked after the design has been completed. Each

Working French knots

backstitch is worked into the same holes in the woven fabric as the previously sewn cross-stitches and can be worked vertically, horizontally or diagonally. From following the diagram it is obvious that each stitch is worked from front to back and is always worked in exactly the same manner, although the direction can change as the outline follows the design.

15

French knots

These small tightly twisted knots are perfect for adding the finishing touches to flowers, for eyes and antenna tips for butterflies or for individual spots of pollen.

To make a French or colonial knot, bring the needle up at A as shown in the diagram on the previous page, twist the thread around the needle once, twice or three times, depending on the size of the knot required, and take the needle down again at B. Notice that B is only a thread or two away from where the needle was brought up through the fabric, so that the knot is formed over these threads. If the needle were to be taken down again in exactly the same hole it was brought up, the knot would pull through to the back of the work and completely disappear.

Straight stitch

Straight stitches are worked in any direction on the fabric and do not necessarily follow the squares or woven rows. They can be of any length or thickness depending on what they represent in the design. For instance, straight stitches sewn around the centre of a gum blossom would need to be fine, using only one strand of cotton, while straight stitches used to denote grass would be sewn with two or three strands. Straight stitches can also represent whiskers, butterfly antennae, flower stamens and grass-tree spikes.

To make a straight stitch, bring the needle up at A, which is at the bottom of the stitch, and take it down again at B.

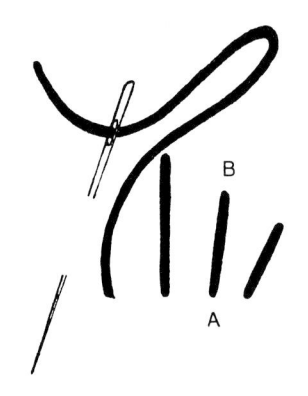

Straight stitches laid randomly on the surface of the fabric

Finishing off stitching

When a length of thread is used up, take the needle and thread behind the work and weave through the backs of seven or eight stitches before cutting away the excess thread. If the needle used to work the cross-stitch has a blunt end, change to a finer, sharp pointed variety to execute this weaving.

Finish working French knots, backstitch and straight stitch simply by taking the needle and thread through to the back of the fabric, working two or three tiny holding stitches into the same place and cutting off the excess thread. Some people prefer to also weave the end of the thread through the backs of a few stitches for security.

WASTE CANVAS

Waste canvas is woven especially for use with closely woven or interlocked fabrics such as cotton polyester, tee-shirting and fleecy lined materials. The cross-stitch is worked over the top of the waste canvas which is removed once the motif has been completed, leaving evenly worked stitches. Waste canvas is different from other types of canvas in that the threads are bonded together with a soluble glue. It is a white double woven fabric with a distinctive dark blue thread denoting each fifth row of thread and comes in two sizes: 11 double rows per 2.5 cm (1") for larger cross-stitching or 14 double rows per 2.5 cm (1") for finer work.

Cut a square of waste canvas slightly larger than the motif to be cross-stitched onto the fabric. Check that the straight grain of the waste canvas is aligned with the straight grain of the background material and tack securely into position. Using two or three strands of embroidery floss or one strand of rayon thread, work the cross-stitching through both the waste canvas and the fabric, making sure that the needle is taken up and down into the very centre of each square in the canvas so that each cross-stitch is of uniform size. Use a sharp-pointed needle as a blunt one will pull and tear interlocked fabric.

When the cross-stitching is completed, dampen the whole motif, including the canvas square. This will have the effect of dissolving the glue which has been holding the canvas threads together. Using tweezers, gently pull out the threads one at a time until only the cross-stitched motif remains.

> *Thread guide for waste canvas*
>
> *11 count:*
>   3 strands embroidery cotton
>   1 strand DMC Perle 5
>
> *14 count:*
>   2 strands embroidery cotton
>   1 strand flower thread
>   1 strand Gumnut silk
>   1 strand cotton with 1 strand Rajmahal art silk
>   2 strands blending filament with 1 strand art silk

Simple kookaburra design worked on waste canvas

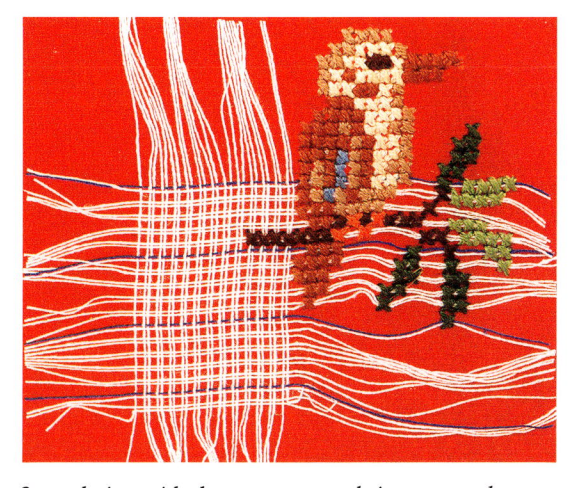

Same design with the waste canvas being removed

PERFORATED PAPER

Perforated paper is a thin stiff card which has tiny holes punched into it at regular intervals, making it suitable for cross-stitch and embroidery. Modern perforated paper is manufactured in a large range of colours, from white, cream and natural to Christmas red, green, gold and silver. The holes are punched in rows of 14 to each 2.5 cm (1") of card, corresponding to 14 HPI cross-stitch fabric.

Cross-stitch on this type of card became popular in the 1840s and reached fad proportions by the 1890s, when the era of Victorian sentimentality reached its peak. The method of embroidery was referred to as punchwork. Because the background card did not require filling in with stitches, needlework on perforated paper was quick and inexpensive and highly suitable for small projects such as bookmarks, photograph mounts and greeting cards. These were generally embellished with messages and mottos accompanied by typical Victorian motifs including clasped hands, roses and forget-me-nots, doves of peace and hearts.

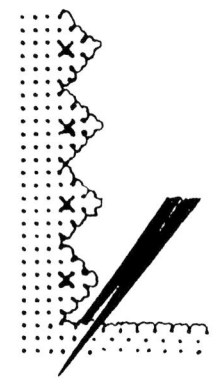

Cutting the edges of perforated paper using very fine sharp-pointed scissors. As the punched holes form the corners of the squares, cut from hole to hole

Many original perforated paper projects are still preserved in museums and private collections and include 'In Memoriam' cards worked in black thread on white paper, bookmarks with lacy designs cut out of the edge of the paper, calling cards and needlecase covers.

SILK AND RAYON THREADS

Embroidery with silk, rayon or silk/viscose mixed threads is similar to using other types of threads. These threads, however, do tend to contain a certain amount of 'spring', and require winding onto plastic or cardboard floss-cards before use. To wind the thread onto the card, pull off the endpaper and open the skein into a circle. Place this circle of silk or rayon thread over the right wrist (left wrist for left-handers) and insert the end into the slit in the threadholder. Wind evenly and slowly away from the body, turning the wrist whenever the thread becomes tight.

Rayon, silk or mixed fibre threads which have a greater degree of spring in them than the normal stranded cotton may need to be 'calmed down' while you are working with them, particularly if you have more than one strand in the needle. A single thread may loop in the needle, leaving the other threads to pull through smoothly, or one thread may form a knot while the others remain straight. These problems can be both frustrating and annoying but there are solutions: you can run a slightly damp cloth along the length of sewing thread, run the thread along the edge of a beeswax block or spray the threads very sparingly with spray starch and iron them.

When threading a needle with two threads, cut one strand double the required length and thread one end through the eye of the needle. Hold both cut ends together and pull gently until the loop of the thread is in the eye. While this method involves commencing the embroidery with a tail of excess thread which must be caught behind the fabric with the first few stitches, it does help both lengths of silk or rayon to slide through the material smoothly. This method is not recommended for competitive cross-stitch because the twists of the two lengths of thread will be running in opposite directions, but it is quite satisfactory in normal situations.

To maintain the lustre of silk or rayon embroidery, dry-cleaning is preferable to washing. If bleeding of the dyes does occur, simply rinse in cold water to which a little bicarbonate of soda or vinegar has been added. Continue rinsing until no residual dye remains.

FLOWER THREADS WITH LINEN

Flower thread is a single-stranded cotton thread which has been designed to work extremely well with linen. While the subtle colours blend together harmoniously and the even tension of the cross-stitch looks beautiful, there is a certain amount of careful preparation required before commencing the actual embroidery.

Flower threads are sold in skeins similar to stranded cotton but containing almost three times the length of thread. For this reason, flower thread must be wound onto floss-cards first. A knot in nearly 20 metres (22 yards) of cotton will cause the utmost frustration and will probably end up in the bin!

To wind the cotton onto the holder, hold the skein in one hand and pull the paper wrappers down towards the bottom end—do not pull them off completely. Now find the centre of the threads at the top end by gradually looping each single thread over one hand. When every loop of thread has been placed over the hand and the centre of the skein has been found (this can take time and patience), pull the wrappers off the bottom end.

Holding the plastic or cardboard floss-holder in one hand, put the end of the thread into the slit in the card and begin winding slowly and evenly. Periodically unwrap more thread from around the wrist. If a knot appears while you are winding, loosen the threads and the knot and weave the floss-holder through the threads until it is free again.

Continue winding until all the thread is neatly on the holder and secure the end into the second slit. Make a note of each colour code number on the end of the appropriate holder.

BEADED CROSS-STITCH

The addition of small glass beads to a cross-stitched project can give a very attractive three-dimensional finish. Beading is particularly suitable for the centres of flowers, the pollen around the edge of a gum blossom, or water droplets on a leaf; the whole cross-stitched motif can be beaded if you like.

There are three methods of attaching beads to cross-stitch; one is more suitable for use with individual beads while the other two are used to cover solid areas within a design.

Method 1
When beads are merely dotted around on the surface of the fabric they are attached after the entire cross-stitch embroidery has been completed. Bring the needle up at the bottom of the square where the bead is to be sewn, thread the bead onto the needle and take the needle down at the top of the square. If the beads are to lie diagonally on the fabric, bring the needle up at the bottom left corner of the square before threading on the bead and taking it down through the fabric at the top right corner.

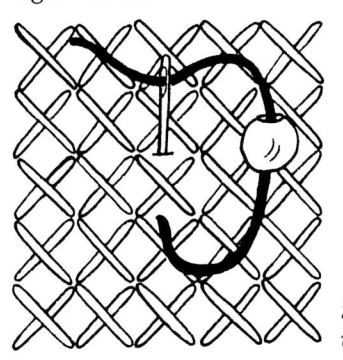

Sewing an individual bead to worked cross-stitch

Method 2
This method is used when the beads are required to lie vertically on the fabric and are sewn into the design as each complete cross-stitch is formed. As the first half of the stitch is made, slip the bead over the needle before the thread is taken down at the top right hand corner. Bring the needle out again at the bottom right corner of the stitch, thread the needle through the bead again and complete the stitch by taking the needle down through the fabric at the top left-hand corner.

Method 3
Complete the first half of a row of cross-stitches, then bring the needle up at the right-hand bottom corner in preparation for working the second or top half of each

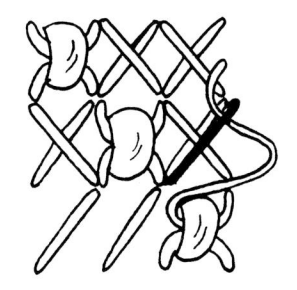

Sewing beads using method 2

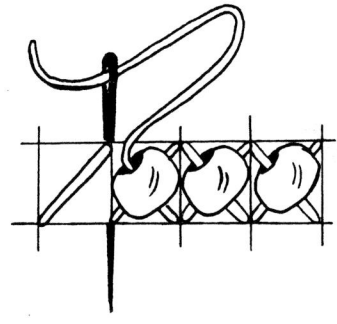

Laying beads at an angle

stitch. Thread the bead over the needle before taking the thread down at the top left-hand corner, and repeat along row. This method means that the beads will be slanted slightly to the right.

VARIEGATED THREADS

There are two types of variegated threads. In the first, the thread is dyed in varying shades of a single colour. DMC and Anchor both produce single-coloured variegated threads which are useful for working flower petals and leaves, shaded fur and feathers, grass and sky.

In the second type, which includes the Minnamurra range, each skein of thread is overdyed in several subtle colours. One skein may graduate from yellow through greens and blues to purple; while these threads need to be used carefully, they can be included to great effect in original and creative designs.

While these variegated threads can be used in exactly the same manner as normal stranded cotton, this can lead to an individual cross-stitch having the first or bottom stitch worked in one shade or colour, with the second or top stitch being in another, thus defeating the idea of subtly changing hues.

Two other methods of working with variegated threads both give better results; it is entirely the decision of the embroiderer which one is used.

Method 1
Draw out the desired number of threads from the six strands and complete each cross-stitch one at a time. In this way the entire stitch is worked in a single colour with the next stitch being a shade lighter or darker. Where several rows are needed, begin sewing a row of complete stitches from left to right. At the end of the row, turn the entire piece of fabric upside down and return along the next row, working again from left to right. This will ensure that the cross-stitches all lie in the same direction.

Method 2
Draw out the desired number of threads from the six strands and work all the bottom halves of a row of cross-stitches across the fabric until the thread has been exhausted. Take the excess thread to the back of the work and weave through the back of the stitches. Thread the needle again, with the thread reversed so that the colours used in the last stitches are now at the end of the thread in position to start the second half of each cross-stitch. Pull the needle through the bottom right-hand side of the last stitch worked, match the colour of that part of the thread, and complete the second or top row of the stitches.

METALLIC THREADS

Most of the major thread companies manufacture metallic and high lustre threads which are suitable for use with cross-stitch projects. Some of these threads can be used alone while others require a holding or strengthening thread such as stranded cotton or art silk to be used with them. Metallic threads can be included in the actual cross-stitch or laid on the surface of the material and couched on once the cross-stitching is complete.

Metallic threads come in a variety of thicknesses and textures which means you have to give some thought to which one is most suitable for your proposed design. Metallic and high lustre threads are conveniently presented on a spool, pre-wound onto a cardboard threadholder or in a pouch where the thread is pulled from the bottom of the pack as required.

It is well worth checking out the different brands before making a decision because of the colour variations in golds and silvers, pearls and colours. DMC, for instance, produce a beautiful antique gold, Rajmahal a soft pale gold and Kreinik a sparkly gold. It is a good idea to keep the various brands, shades and thicknesses of metallic threads stored in a special workbox and to build up a ready supply.

Kreinik Metallics in particular specialise in both metallic and high lustre threads; they supply a complete range of colours and threads, from the very fine blending filament to heavy braids and ribbons. Two strands of blending filaments can be used with a single strand of either stranded cotton or Rajmahal art silk thread to provide a subtle sparkle to embroidery without giving a glittery effect. A glittery look is obtained by using either Kreinik high lustre threads with a single strand of cotton or silk or one of the Madeira or Coats range of synthetic metallic threads.

Blending filaments are extremely fine and durable but because they are used simultaneously with a completely different textured thread, they should be knotted onto the eye of the needle before the holding thread is inserted. To achieve the desired uniformity, cut the blending filament thread twice as long as required. Place the two cut ends together and thread the looped end through the eye, making the loop long enough to thread the needle point into it.

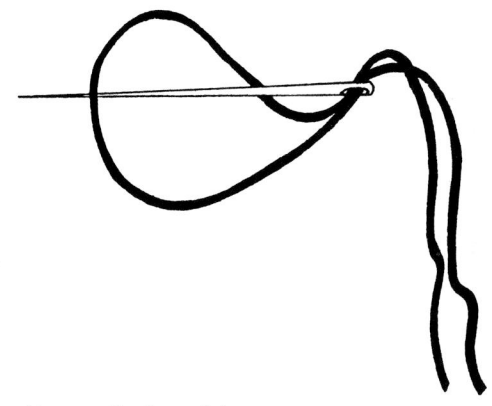

Taking needle through loop

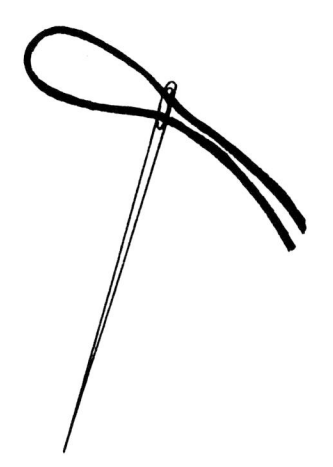

Threading loop through eye of needle

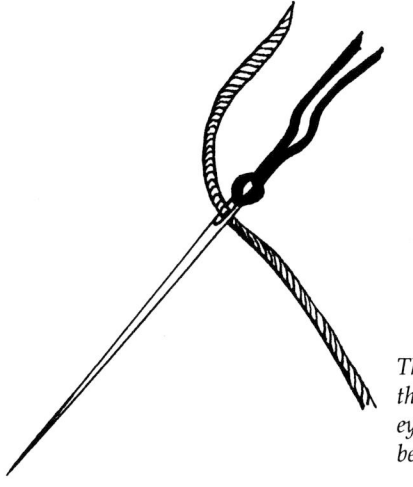

Threading cotton through the needle eye after the loop has been tightened

Once the needle point has been taken through the loop, pull the loop tight to form a knot at the top of the eye. Cut the stranded cotton or art silk thread about 4 cm (1½") longer than the double blending filament and thread through the needle eye.

Fine and medium weight metallic braids are also suitable for use by themselves when the design calls for an area of solid sparkle. Fine braid is used on fabric requiring two strands of cotton, such as Aida 16, and medium braid is suitable for fabrics which require three strands of thread, such as Aida 14 or 11. Braids tend to fray when cut so use the following trick to thread them easily through the eye of the needle: Choose a needle which has a long enough eye to take the braid without twisting it, then cut a tiny piece of paper and fold it in half. Place this folded paper through the eye and open the end so that the braid can be inserted into it. Pull the paper and thread through simultaneously.

Most metallic threads are entirely synthetic and so can be either washed or dry-cleaned satisfactorily. If the embroidery needs to be ironed, use a warm to moderate iron and only on the wrong side of the work. Never use a hot iron on the right side of the work as the heat can take the colour off the metallic thread.

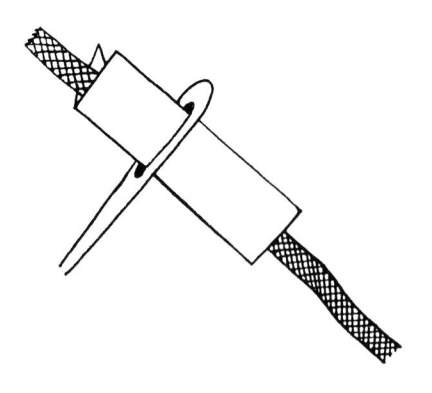

Threading braid and folded paper through eye of needle

SILK GAUZE

Silk gauze is an extremely finely woven fabric suitable for working cross-stitch which is intended to be inserted into miniature jewellery frames or the lids of tiny ring boxes or used on doll's house accessories. It is woven in several different thread counts, the number of threads per 2.5 cm (1") ranging from 28 to 52; I find it is easiest to work with the help of a magnifying glass hung around the neck!

Obviously only a single strand of embroidery cotton or silk is required and the fabric needs to be tightly stretched to maintain an even tension. Silk gauze is only obtainable from specialist embroidery stores and is rather expensive, making it uneconomical to think of working large pieces.

To hold a small square of gauze (or even fine Aida cloth or linen) taut in an embroidery hoop, it must be sewn onto a larger piece of calico or cotton fabric. Place this backing fabric in the hoop and stretch it tight. Slip stitch the smaller square of fabric onto the centre of the larger piece with small even stitches which are strong enough to support the edges firmly. Carefully cut away the backing fabric from behind the gauze and work the cross-stitched motif. Once the embroidery is complete, remove the holding stitches and mount the finished project.

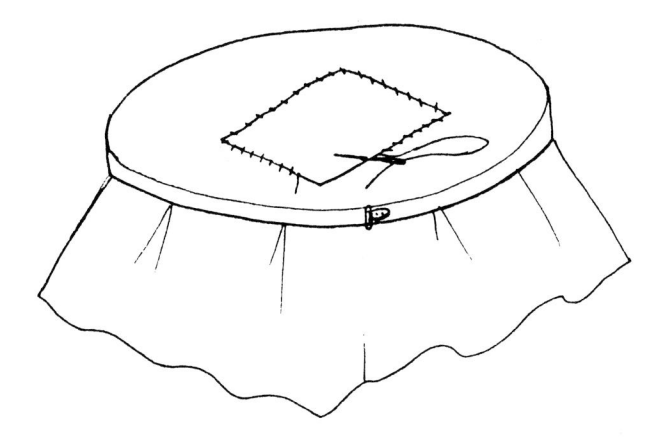

Stitching gauze to backing or holding fabric

BORDERS AND MONOGRAMS

Borders

Border patterns can be designed as an individual motif which is intended to be worked along a strip of fabric, as one single pattern which is simply repeated along the length of the border or as mirror-imaged motifs which are worked from the centre.

Many fabrics have been woven especially to accommodate cross-stitched borders, but a strip of any evenly woven cotton or linen can be sewn onto a background fabric such as towelling or coloured cotton. Aida band is woven with 14 threads per 2.5 cm (1") of fabric and is available in three different widths: 8 cm (3"), 4.5 cm (1¾") and 2.2 cm (7/8"). It is generally white or cream in colour with scalloped edges in pastel shades of pink, blue, lemon and mauve, vivid red, royal and navy blue, emerald green, black, burgundy, grey/green, chocolate brown and metallic silver and gold. It also comes in plain white on white and cream on cream edging and fabric.

Ready-made items such as handtowels, babies' bibs, napkins and bunny-rugs often have a border of simple squared fabric woven across them which is intended for the inclusion of a cross-stitched border.

Monograms

When sewing a monogram onto a strip of Aida band or a length of Aida cloth or linen, it is important to centre the letters of the name or initials (including full-stops and spaces). If sewing a set of initials, allow one blank space, one full-stop then two more blank spaces between each letter, and one space and full-stop after the final letter. If the monogram is to be placed between two motifs, allow at least three spaces at each end of the monogram to separate the letters from the pattern.

To find the centre of the monogram, count the number of stitches and blank spaces across the name or initials and divide by two. If the total is an even number, run a line of tacking stitches down the centre with half the stitches on either side of this line. If the total is an odd number, run the tacking stitches down the central row, leaving the balance of the stitches evenly placed on either side.

To centre the monogram horizontally on the Aida strip, count the stitches vertically in the letters and divide by two. Once again run a row of tacking stitches through the middle of the fabric. Tack a line around the outside edge of the monogram position before commencing the actual embroidery and work within these guidelines. Remove these tacking stitches once the embroidery is complete.

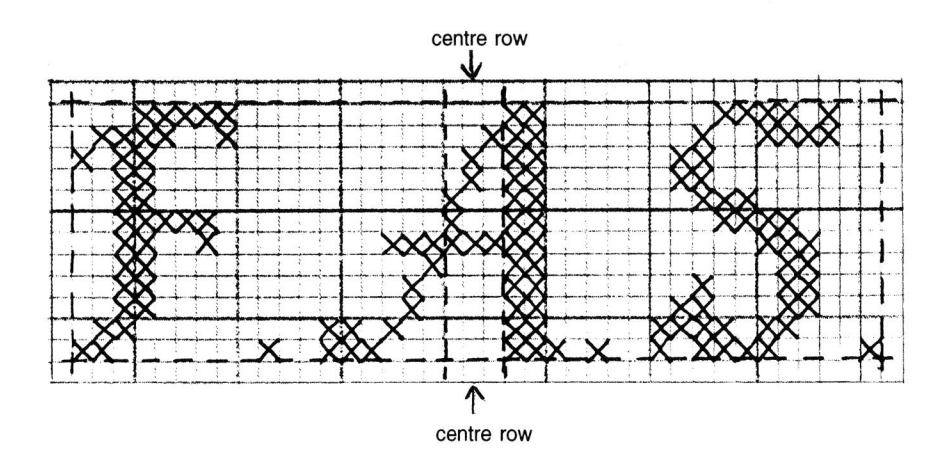

Example of monogram with spaces, 39 stitches wide. There are 19 stitches on either side of the central row

BORDERS AND MONOGRAMS

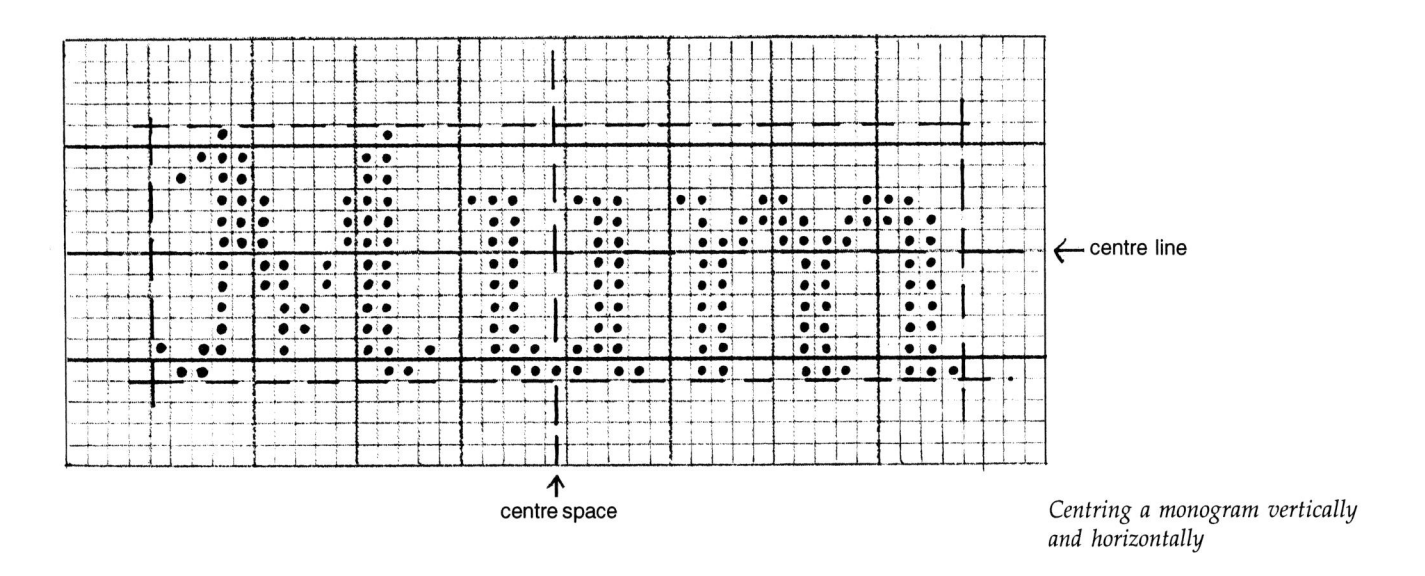

← centre line

↑ centre space

Centring a monogram vertically and horizontally

PAINTED BACKGROUNDS

A creative and totally original effect can be achieved by dyeing or painting the embroidery fabric before working the cross-stitched motif. There are many different dyes and fabric paints on the market and each one comes with individual instructions; however, the following methods have been tried and proven satisfactory. For an item that is to be washed over and over, such as a tee-shirt or hand-towel, use a cold water dye, but for a framed picture water-soluble paints or pencils work extremely well.

Fabric paints

These are available from craft shops in small plastic bottles or tubes and can be used directly from the container without diluting.

To obtain the glow of a sunset for a silhouette picture, to give a particular example, start with a bright yellow Aida fabric. Soak the fabric and lay on a flat surface. Squeeze out dabs of red, purple and orange fabric paint onto a palette and brush streaks of colour across the fabric using an old toothbrush. Begin with the purple at the top, blending into red in the middle and finally orange at the bottom of the area to be worked. Hang on a line to dry so that the colours blend together even more. Follow the same principles for other background effects.

Water-soluble pencils

These pencils are available from art suppliers in boxes of twelve or twenty-four colours.

For definite lines such as hills, fields or golden paddocks, simply draw onto the wet fabric with a wet-tipped pencil, then brush over gently with a soft brush to fill in the designated areas with colour.

The second method of applying colour, where a more diffused appearance is required, is to hold the point of the pencil 5 cm (2") above the wet fabric and brush over the tip with a very wet foam brush (available from folk art/decoupage suppliers) and allow the paint to drip onto the material and the colours to blend together. While these colours are not as resistant as dyes, once they have dried and been heat-set with an iron they are quite satisfactory.

Folk art paints with textile medium

This combination provides a permanently coloured, washable background fabric. Pre-wash the Aida cloth or linen to remove any dressing and other chemicals, then lay flat on a wax-paper covered board. Mix 1 part textile medium to 2 parts folk art paint and, using a stiff-bristled fabric brush, paint the background design, making sure to blend the colours together slightly so as not to create definite lines of colour.

For a subtle, blotchy effect simply sponge the colours onto the fabric, once again taking care to blend the colours slightly where they overlap. Air-dry the fabric for 24 hours before heat-setting with a dry moderate iron.

CARE AND LAUNDERING

It is, of course, preferable to keep your fabric spotlessly clean during the working process so that laundering is not necessary. Always keep your hands clean, especially on warm days when grease and perspiration tend to build up on the fingers, by washing them frequently with warm soapy water. Dry them thoroughly and sprinkle a little talcum powder into your palms to keep them fresh.

Another thing which tends to mark the fabric is the embroidery hoop. Whenever the embroidery is being put away for the day, remove the hoop first. Apart from avoiding a circular crease in the fabric, it also prevents the seemingly permanently marked circle caused by dust and grease.

Unfortunately, there will always be the odd occasion when grubby hands, dusty embroidery hoops or, worst of all, a tea or coffee drip, make washing necessary. Fill a basin or large bowl with warm (not hot) water and soft soap flakes (not detergent) and work up a frothy lather. Holding the material straight between the hands, dip it in the water and swish it in an up and down motion so that the bubbles can penetrate the fabric.

Never wring the fabric before rinsing. Lay it on a flat cloth and fill the basin with cold clean water. Once again, dip the material up and down until the soap is removed. Lay a towel flat, place the fabric on top of the towel and carefully roll it tightly to squeeze out the water. The reason the work is rolled in this manner is to keep it free from wrinkles as much as possible, as 100% cottons and linens tend to hold stubborn creases.

Unroll the towel and lay it with the fabric on top to dry out, away from direct sunlight which will fade some colours, especially reds and blues. If the embroidery has become distorted and out of shape during the laundering, gently tug the corners square and pin it in shape to the towel while it dries.

Once the material is completely dry, lay a padded surface such as a folded sheet or towel onto the ironing board. Dampen the fabric with a fine spray, lay it face-down onto the padding and iron it on the wrong side with a moderately hot iron. If the cross-stitching is ironed directly, on the right side of the work, the stitches will become flattened and twisted.

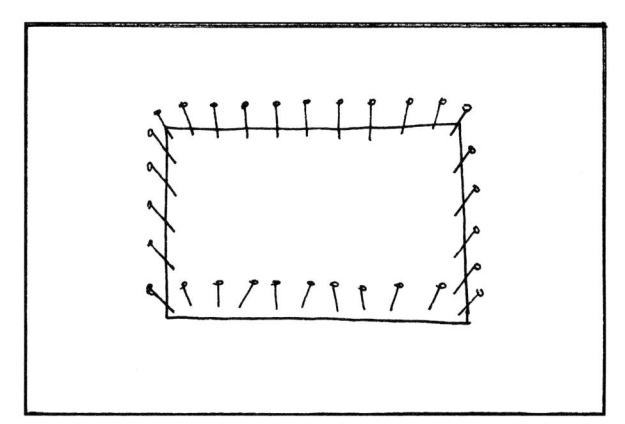

Rolling the fabric in a towel to squeeze out excess water

Fabric pinned out to dry evenly stretched

PREPARING WORK FOR FRAMING

To prepare the completed cross-stitch for framing cut a piece of backing board to the required size and cover with a sheet of 1 mm thick wadding or Pellon. Lay the material over this padding and, making sure that the motif is centred correctly, lace the fabric firmly across the back of the board. Begin at the centre and work from one side to the other until one end is secure. Repeat from the centre to the other end of the fabric. Fold the two free ends over to the back and cut away any excess fabric at the corners before lacing firmly from top to bottom.

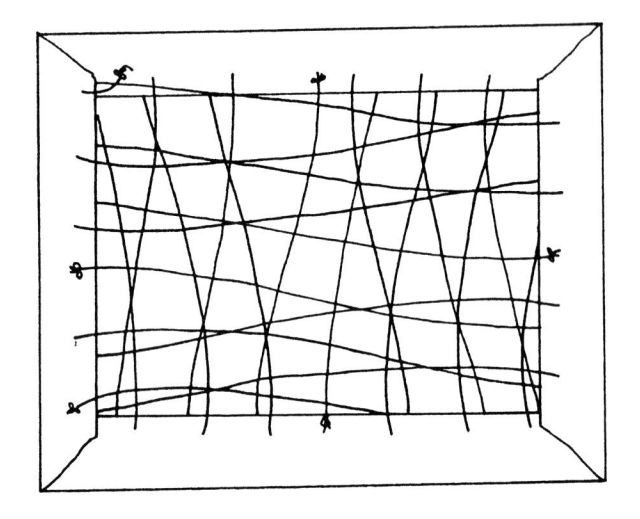

Lacing the work from the centre, working outwards

Cross-stitch laced and ready for framing

DESIGN PORTFOLIO

This collection of designs is intended to be used as reference material. Each design can be sewn over waste canvas, trimmed with beading, worked with highlights of metallic threads, cross-stitched onto hand-painted fabric or simply embroidered with stranded cotton or flower threads. The designs can be varied, used in part and, remember, at any size you want.

Thread and fabric guide

Aida 11 HPI:
   3 or 4 strands cotton or silk
   3 strands DMC rayon
   4 strands Rajmahal rayon

Aida 14 HPI:
   2 or 3 strands cotton or silk
   2 strands DMC rayon
   3 strands Rajmahal art silk
   2 strands Kreinik blending filament with 1 strand cotton or art silk

Aida 16 HPI:
   1 or 2 strands cotton or silk
   1 strand DMC rayon
   2 strands Rajmahal art silk
   2 strands Kreinik blending filament with 1 strand art silk

Aida 18 HPI:
   1 or 2 strands cotton or silk
   1 strand Rajmahal art silk
   1 strand Kreinik blending filament with 1 strand art silk

Hardanger 22 HPI:
   Stitch over two threads and treat as 11 count Aida fabric.

Linen 25HPI and 32HPI:
Always work over two threads of weave.
   2 strands cotton or silk
   1 strand flower thread
   1 strand DMC rayon
   2 strands Rajmahal art silk
   1 strand art silk and 2 strands blending filament

SOURCEBOOK FOR AUSTRALIAN CROSS-STITCH

Platypus sewn with three strands of cotton onto a commercial placemat using the waste canvas method with 14 HPI canvas

WASTE CANVAS

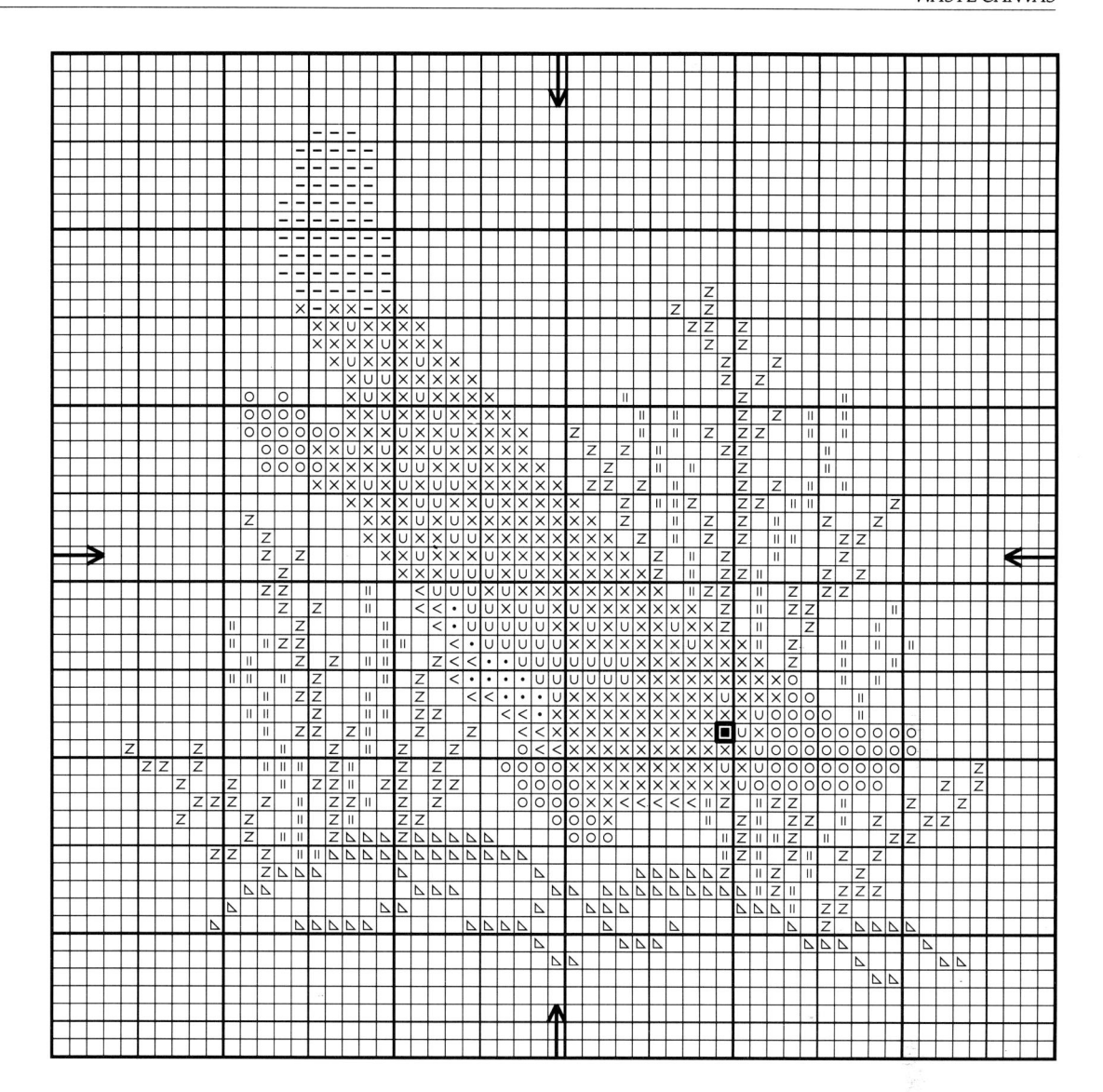

Platypus Key

DMC Threads

- ■ 310 Black
- − 3787 Dark Taupe
- X 839 Dark Brown
- O 413 Grey
- < 3774 Pale Peach
- • 712 Cream
- Z 469 Dark Green
- ‖ 3364 Light Green
- ◺ 834 Beige
- U 632 Rust Brown

33

Numbat sewn with three strands of cotton onto a commercial placemat using the waste canvas method with 14 HPI canvas

WASTE CANVAS

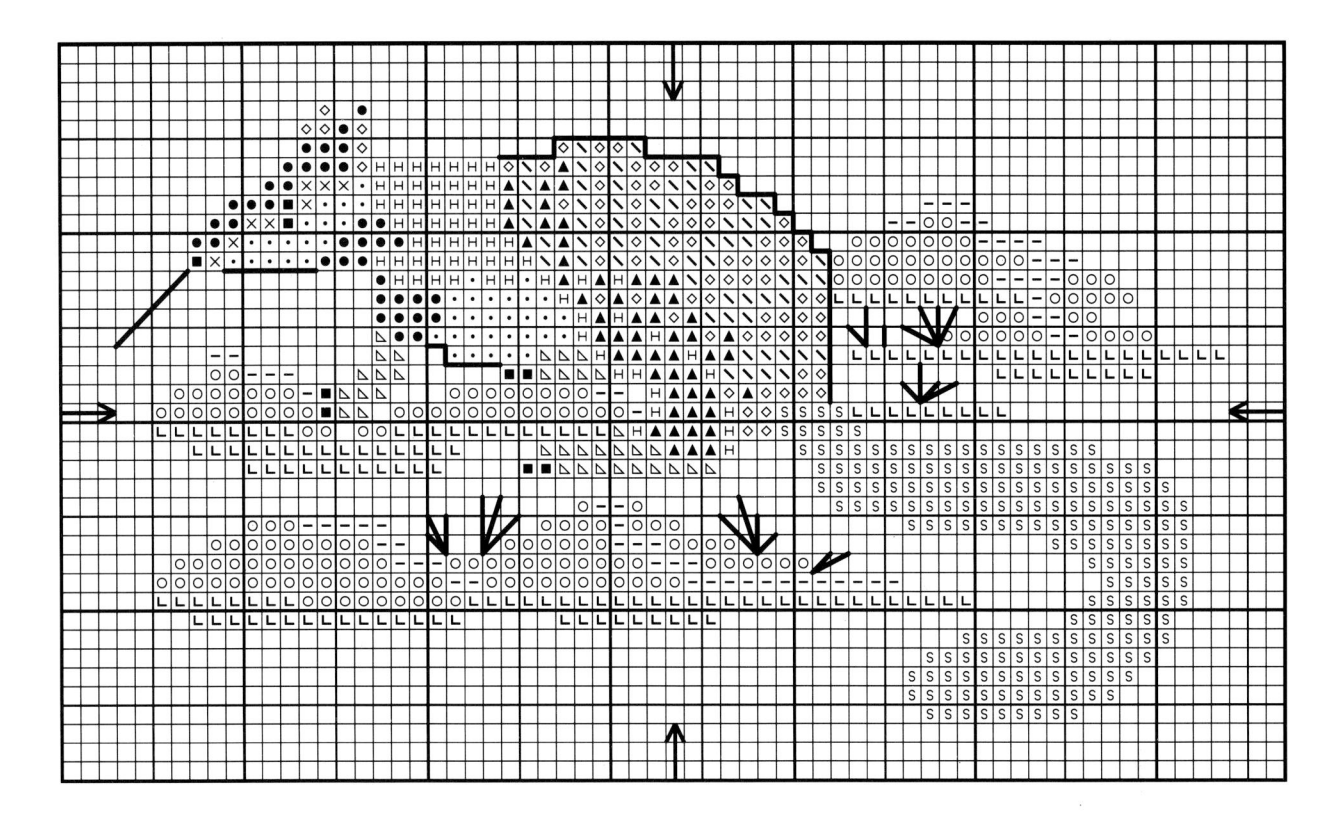

Numbat Key

DMC Stranded Cotton

- ■ 310 Black
- × 3022 Steel Grey
- − 844 Dark Grey
- ○ 318 Light Grey
- ▲ 1 Strand 3826 & 2 Strands 3827
- ● 2 Strands 3826 & 1 Strand 869
- · 951 Pale Peach
- H 2 Strands 869 & 1 Strand 3826
- ◇ 3371 Dark Chocolate
- ◣ 712 Cream
- ◢ 3827 Light Rust
- L 320 Green
- S 2 Strands 3371 & 1 Strand 712
- ⌐ 310 Black
- ⌐ 935 Dark Green

35

The pink heath bookmark is worked with flower threads on perforated paper while the kookaburra card is worked with two strands of stranded cotton

PERFORATED PAPER

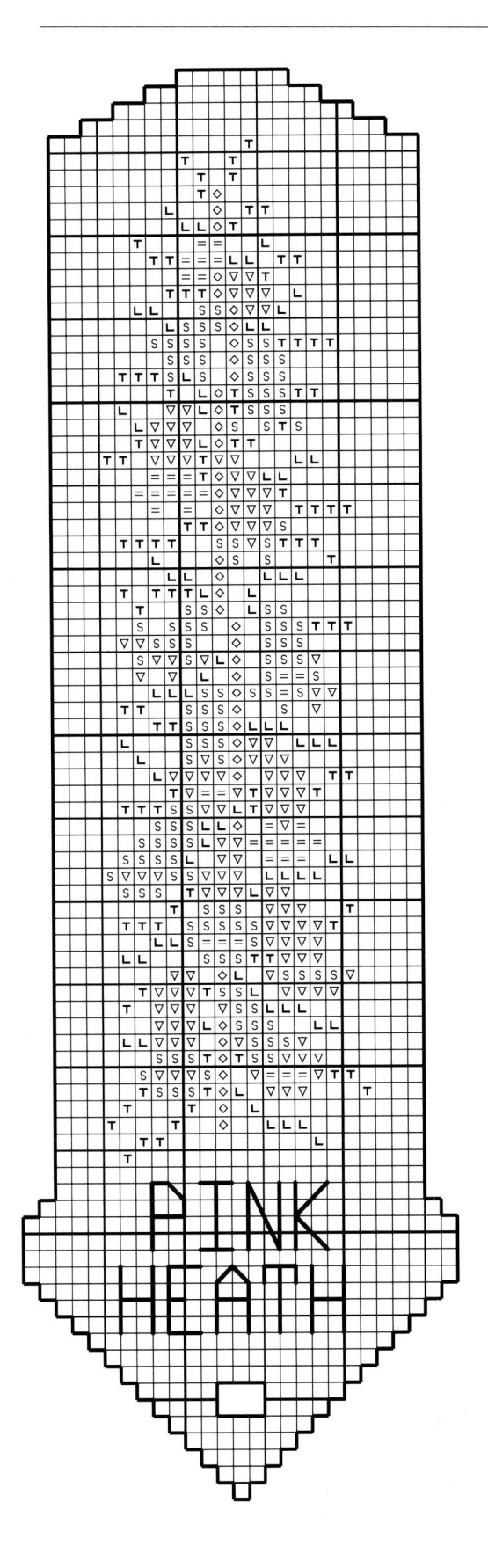

Pink Heath Key

DMC Threads

- ⑤ 2899 Pale Pink
- ▽ 2309 Medium Pink
- = 2326 Deep Pink
- T 2734 Light Green
- L 2469 Dark Green
- ◇ 2434 Brown
- ⌐ 2640 Muddy Brown

Small Kookaburra Key

DMC Stranded Cotton

- ■ 310 Black
- ⊠ 733 Light Green
- ● 469 Dark Green
- ▲ 310/640 1 strand of each
- ⑤ 3766 Blue
- L 3024 Stone
- T 822 Cream
- H 644 Fawn
- ⋂ 3772 Stem
- F 642 Beige
- ⌐ 822 Cream Backstitch

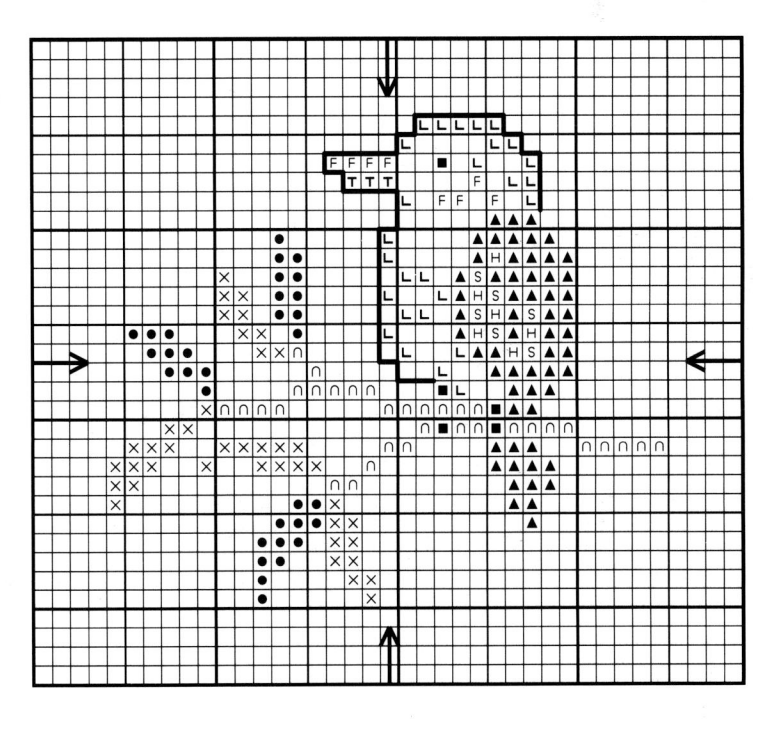

37

SOURCEBOOK FOR AUSTRALIAN CROSS-STITCH

A black swan on a kangaroo paw background is worked on perforated paper in two strands of stranded cotton, with the water being worked with one strand of cotton combined with two strands of Kreinik blending filament

PERFORATED PAPER

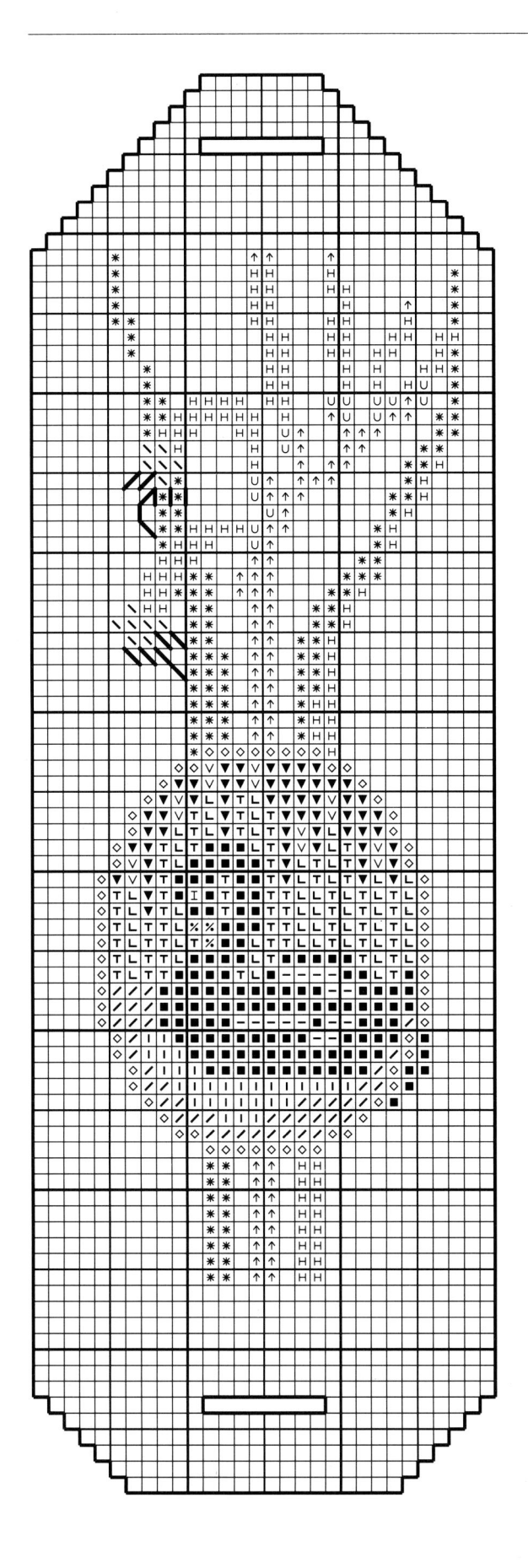

Kangaroo Paw Bookmark Key

DMC Flower Threads

- ■ 2310 Black
- − 2318 Grey
- ✻ 2890 Bottle Green
- H 2905 Emerald
- ↑ 2321 Red
- \ 2446 Yellow
- U 2815 Deep Red
- ◊ 2898 Brown
- V 2918 Rust
- ▼ 2800 Sky Blue
- ⁒ 2740 Orange
- I Blanc White
- T 2905 Light Green
- L 2732 Olive Green
- I 1 Strand 2597 with 2 strands Kreinik Filament
- ∕ 1 Strand 2599 with 2 strands Kreinik Filament
- ⌐ 310 Black Flower Stamen

39

SOURCEBOOK FOR AUSTRALIAN CROSS-STITCH

Red-breasted robin sewn with one strand of DMC rayon thread onto 16 HPI Aida fabric

SILK AND RAYON THREADS

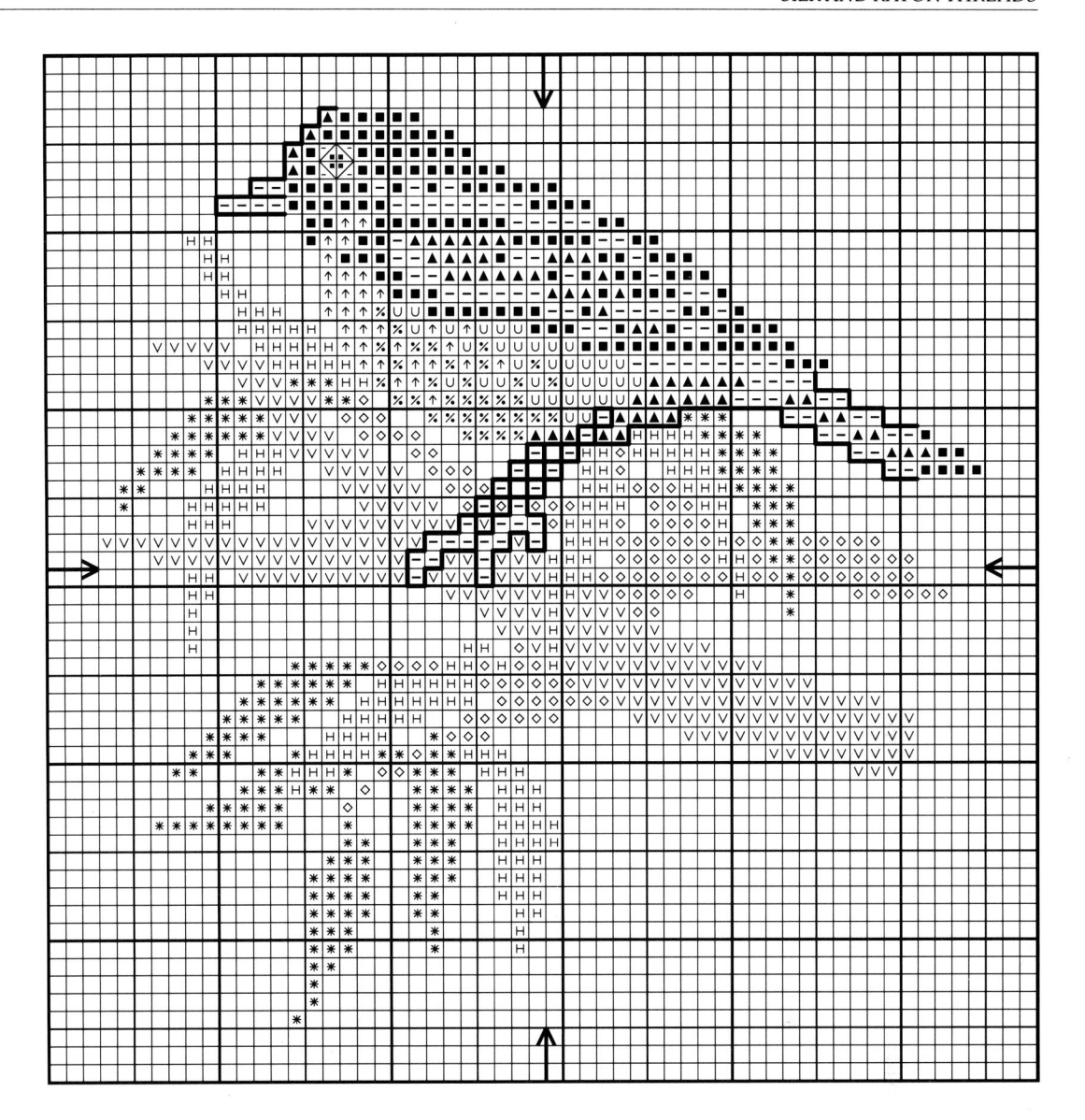

Red Robin Key

DMC Rayon Threads

- ■ R310 Black
- — R415 Light Grey
- ▲ R5200 White
- U R321 Deep Red
- ↑ R349 Bright Red
- % R666 Strawberry Red
- ✱ R469 Deep Green
- H R581 Light Green
- ◊ R3781 Dark Brown
- V R301 Rust
- ⌐ R310 Outline

Shells sewn onto towelling border with single strands of Gumnut Yarns pure silk threads, using the waste canvas method with 16 HPI canvas

Shell Border Key

Gumnut Yarns Silk Threads

U	178	Rose	II	464	Pale Green	◣	746	Gold
+	194	Mauve	⌐	744	Ivory	I	706	Lemon
▽	825	Apricot	◥	966	Buff	◲	486	Aqua
·	863	Beige	✳	969	Dark Brown	◆	786	Orange
◇	949	Brown	↑	827	Coral	▣	746	Old Gold
∨	947	Fawn	S	823	Pink	=	857	Blush Pink
▶	945	Cream	O	994	Silver Grey	◥	784	Pale Apricot
			▲	233	Pale Mauve			

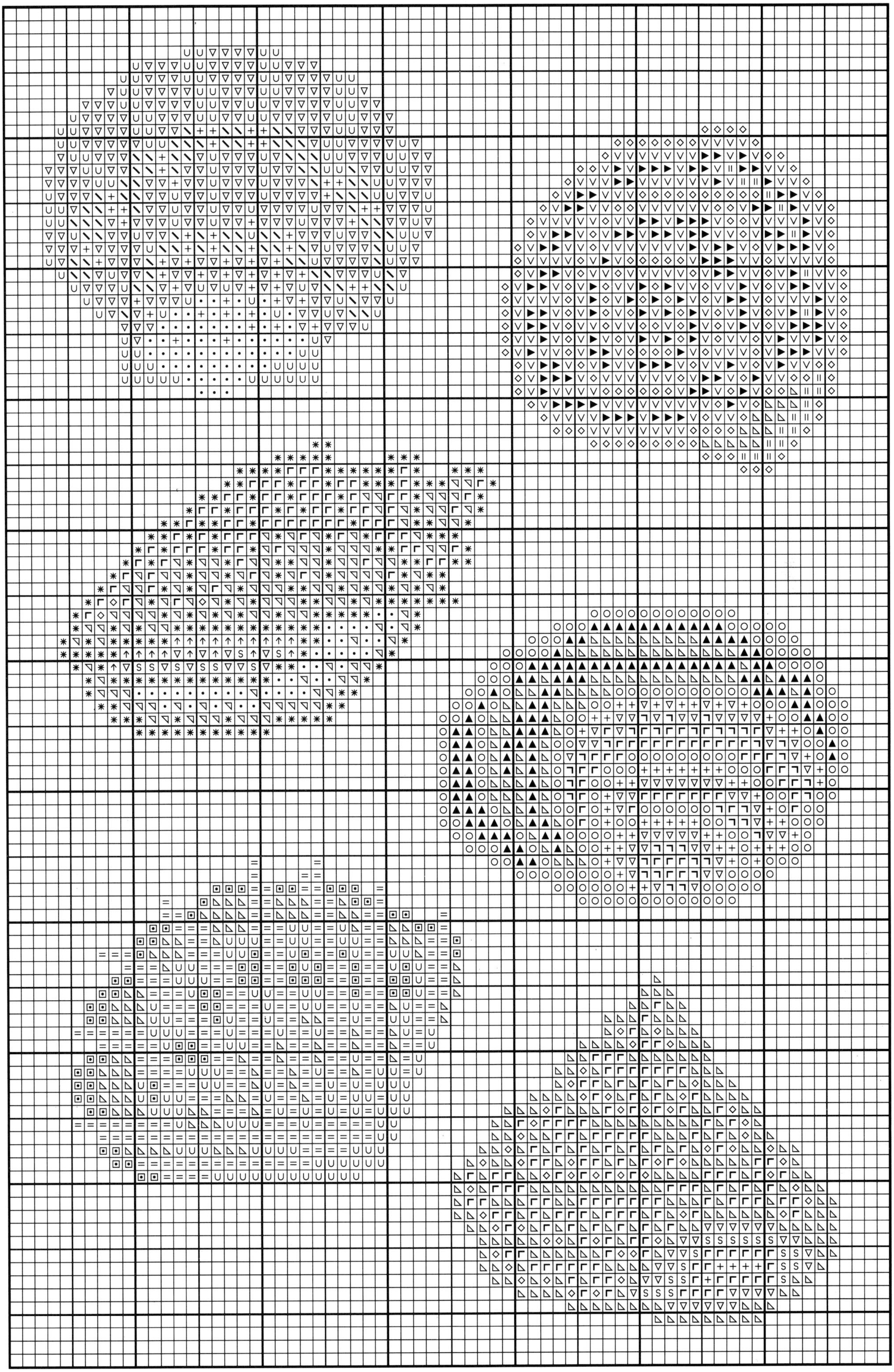

Native berries needle box and pincushion cross-stitched using flower threads over two threads on Belfast linen

FLOWER THREADS WITH LINEN

Native Berries Key

DMC Flower Threads

⌀	2740	Orange
V	2922	Rust
△	2531	Purple
·	2209	Mauve
↑	2666	Bright Red
=	2346	Deep Red
U	2497	Maroon
/	2312	Blue
▼	2322	Light Blue
O	2318	Grey
+	2748	Yellow
→	2745	Lemon
◆	2469	Leaf Green
T	2788	Apple Green
L	2732	Olive Green
▢	2471	Pale Green
Z	2501	Bottle Green
■	2310	Black
⋙	2730	Deep Olive

Straight Stitch Stems

⌐ Red Berries – Black

⌐ Black Berries – Rust

⌐ Orange Berries – Rust

⌐ Dark Red Berries – Bottle Green

⌐ Yellow Berries – Black

Back Stitch Leaf Veins

⌐ Apple Green Leaves – Deep Olive

⌐ Pale Green Leaves – Rust

⌐ Bottle and Leaf Green Leaves – Rust

⌐ Olive Green Leaves – Black

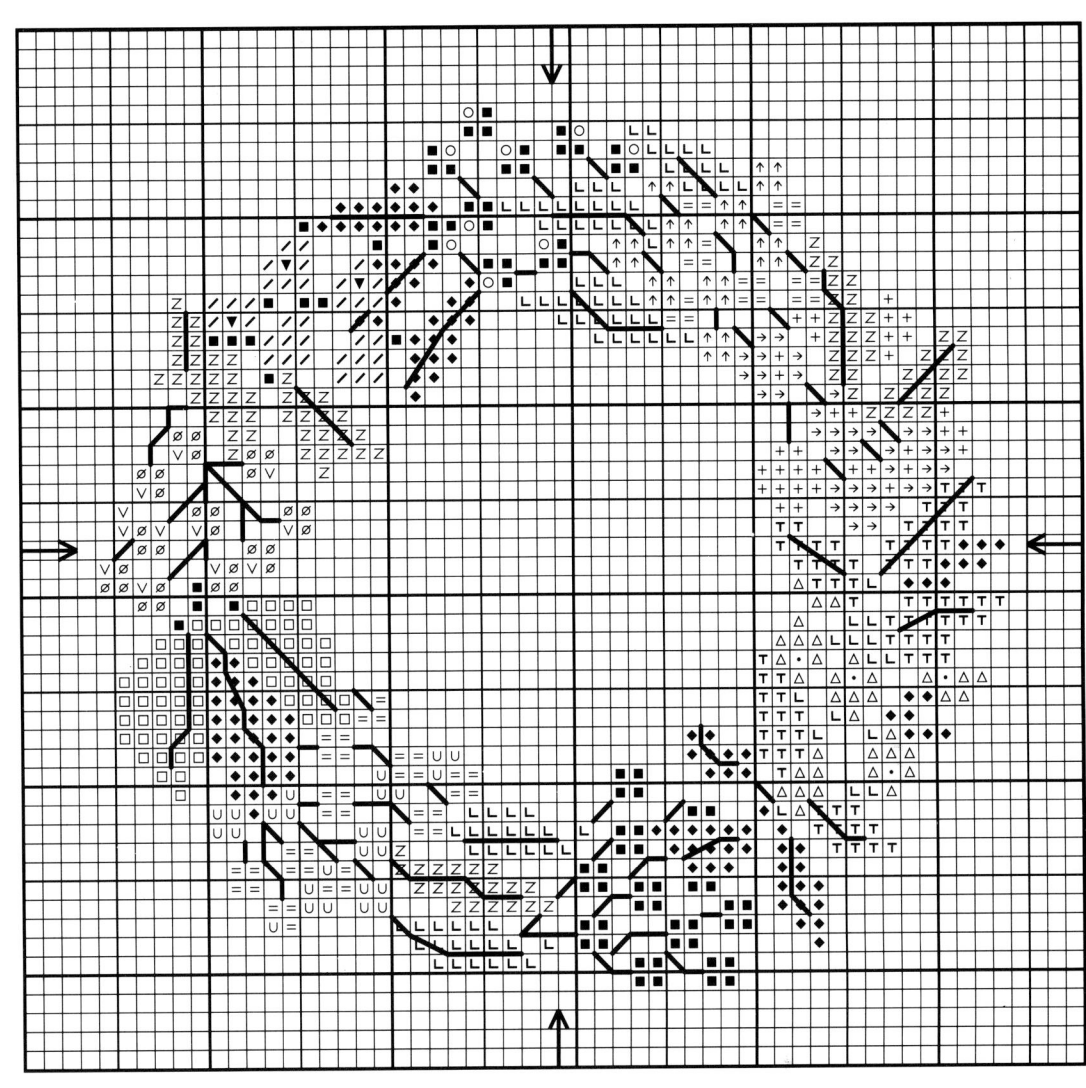

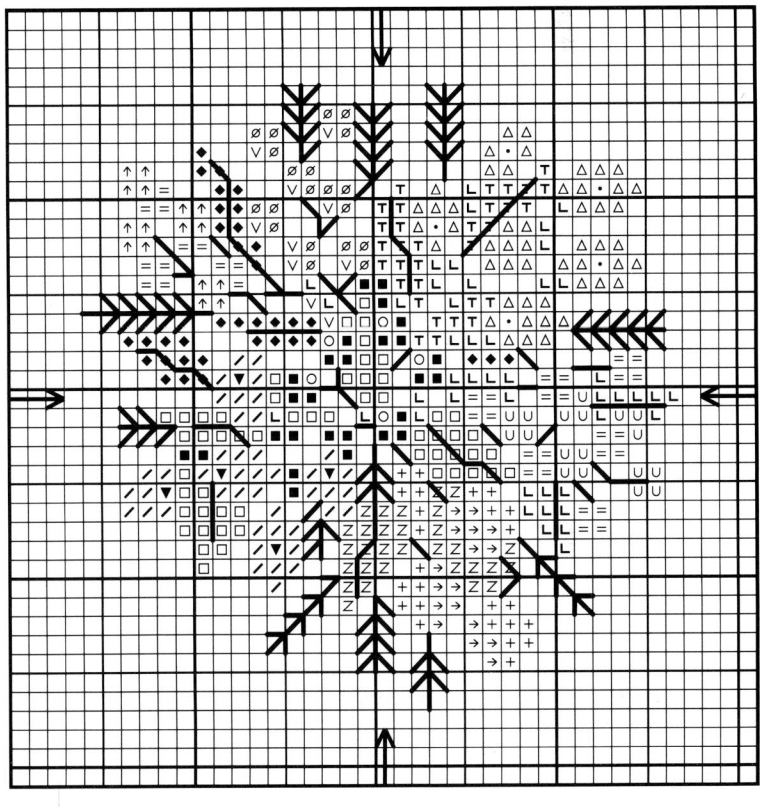

SOURCEBOOK FOR AUSTRALIAN CROSS-STITCH

Native orchid greeting cards worked in flower threads over two threads on Belfast linen

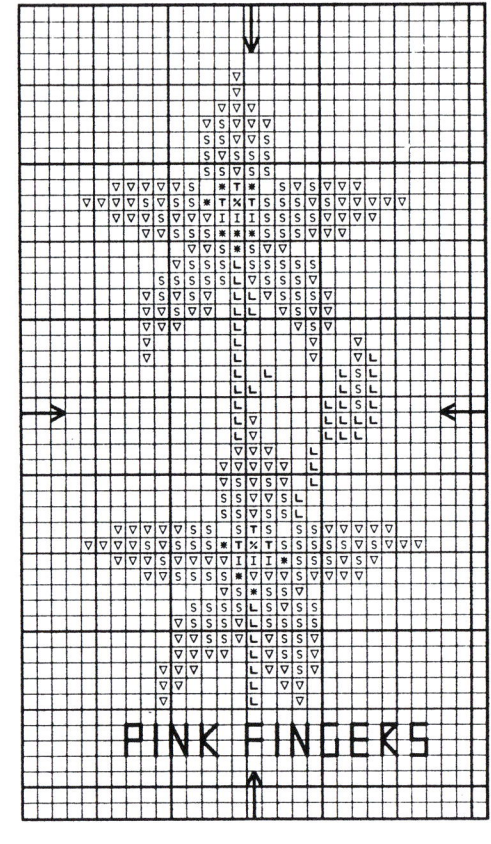

Pink Finger Orchids Key

DMC Flower Threads

Symbol	Code	Colour
▽	2761	Pink
S	2708	Bright Pink
✱	2899	Deep Pink
T	2734	Light Green
╱	2766	Tan
L	2730	Dark Green
I	2745	Lemon
⌐	2371	Lettering Brown

FLOWER THREADS WITH LINEN

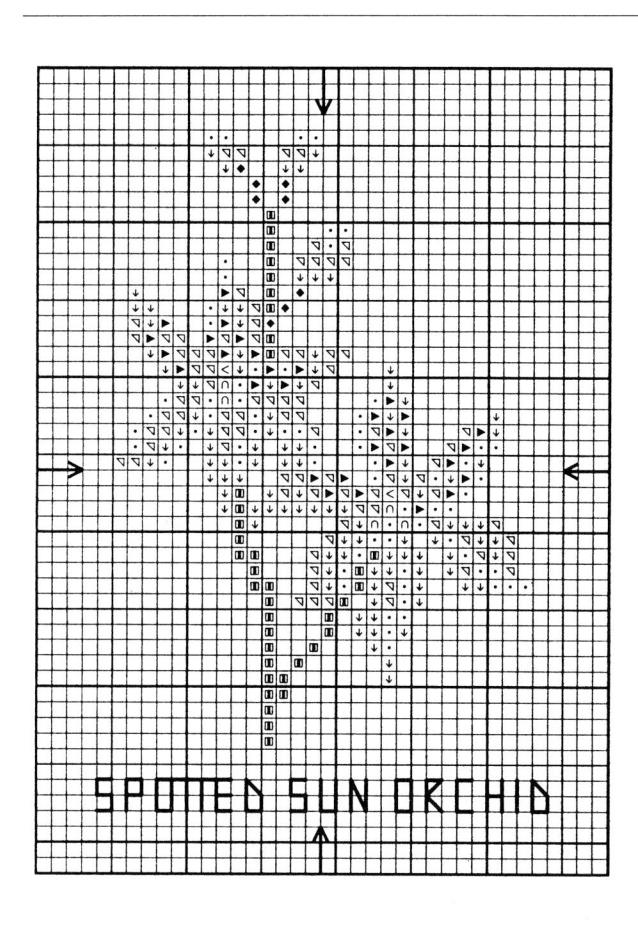

Spotted Sun Orchid Key

DMC Flower Threads

- ⊡ 2395 Lilac
- ↓ 2211 Pale Mauve
- ◸ 2210 Mauve
- ▶ 2394 Dark Purple
- ⊞ 2436 Camel
- ⋂ 2446 Pale Green
- ◆ 2502 Green
- < 2356 Terracotta
- ⌐ 2371 Lettering Brown

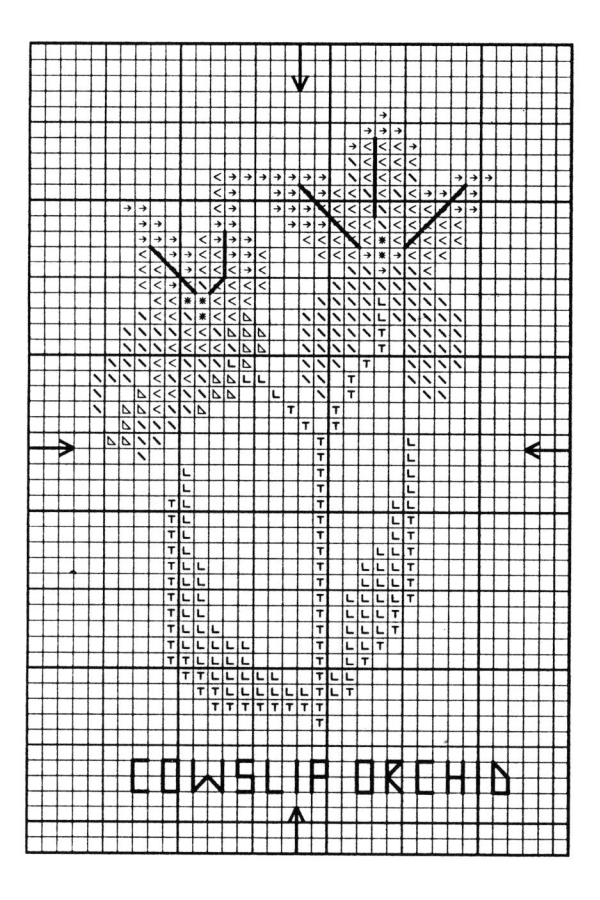

Cowslip Orchid Key

DMC Flower Threads

- → 2743 Medium Yellow
- < 2748 Bright Yellow
- ◸ 2742 Golden Yellow
- T 2471 Light Green
- L 2469 Dark Green
- ✻ 2734 Light Olive
- ◳ 2833 Beige
- ⌐ 2371 Lettering Brown
- ⌐ 2349 Red Veins

Graphs and keys for the Blue Sun Orchid and the Donkey Orchid appear on page 104

Beaded seahorse sewn in three strands of stranded cotton onto 14 HPI Aida fabric painted with diluted folk art paints in green, lime, turquoise and yellow

BEADED CROSS-STITCH

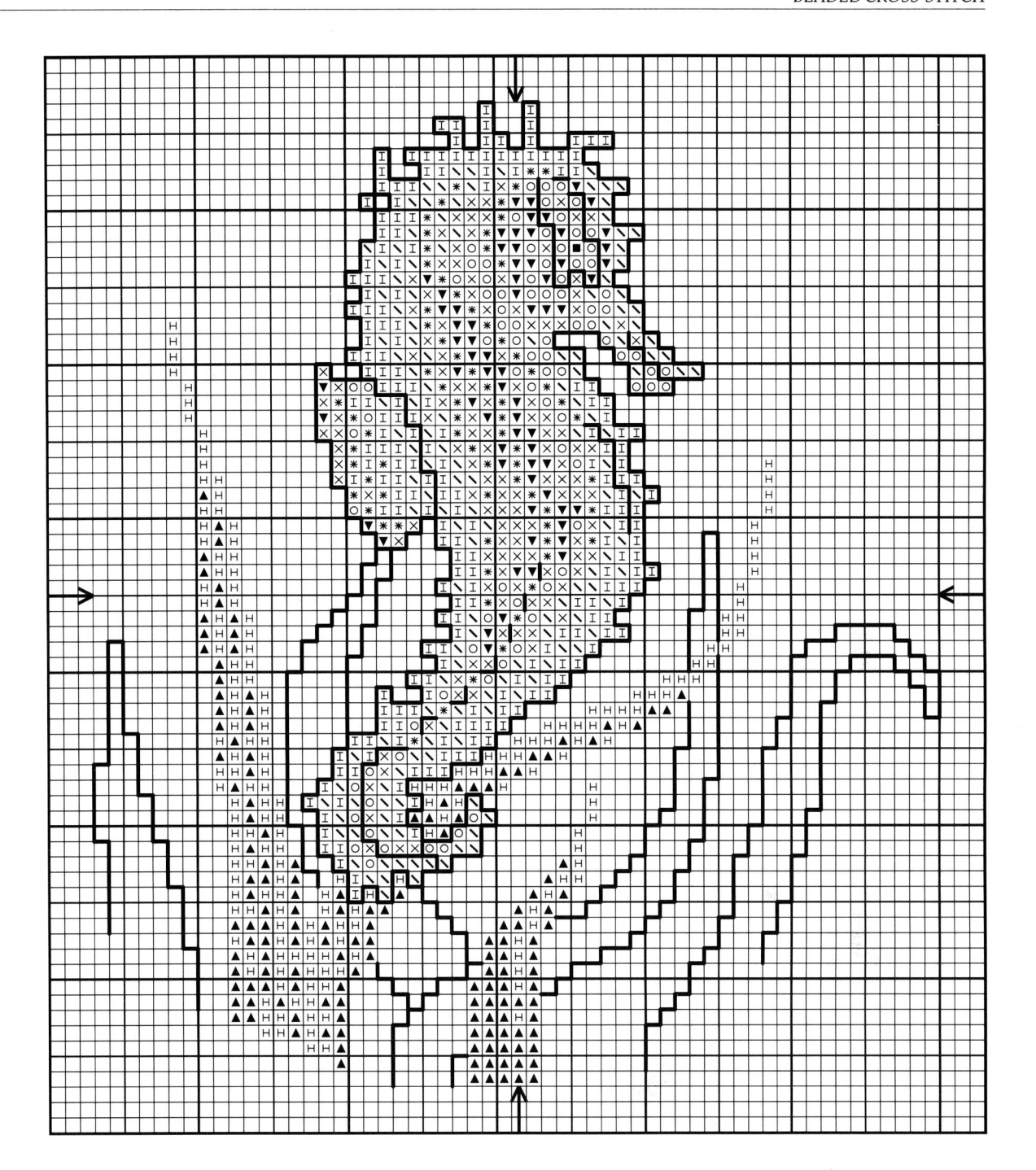

Seahorse Key

DMC Threads

- ■ 310 Black
- ＼ 744 Yellow
- I 746 Pale Yellow
- ▼ 3776 Tan
- O 742 Gold
- X 740 Orange
- ▲ 831 Deep Olive Green
- H 581 Green
- ⌐ 801 Outline Seahorse
- ⌐ 937 Outline Seagrass
- ✽ Mill Hill Bead No. 03036

SOURCEBOOK FOR AUSTRALIAN CROSS-STITCH

Red gum blossom sewing accessories worked with two strands of Rajmahal art silk threads onto cream 16 HPI Aida cloth and finished with red glass seed beads. The straight stitch flowers are worked in single strands

Gum Blossoms Key

	Rajmahal	DMC Stranded Cotton	
◢	805	367	Dark Green
·	421	3364	Light Green
B	841	841	Brown
X	255	304	Red
L	521	470	Lime Green
●	91	744	Yellow French knots

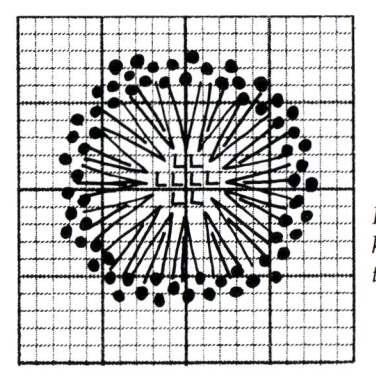

Position of random French knots or seed beads sewn around the straight-stitched flower

50

BEADED CROSS-STITCH

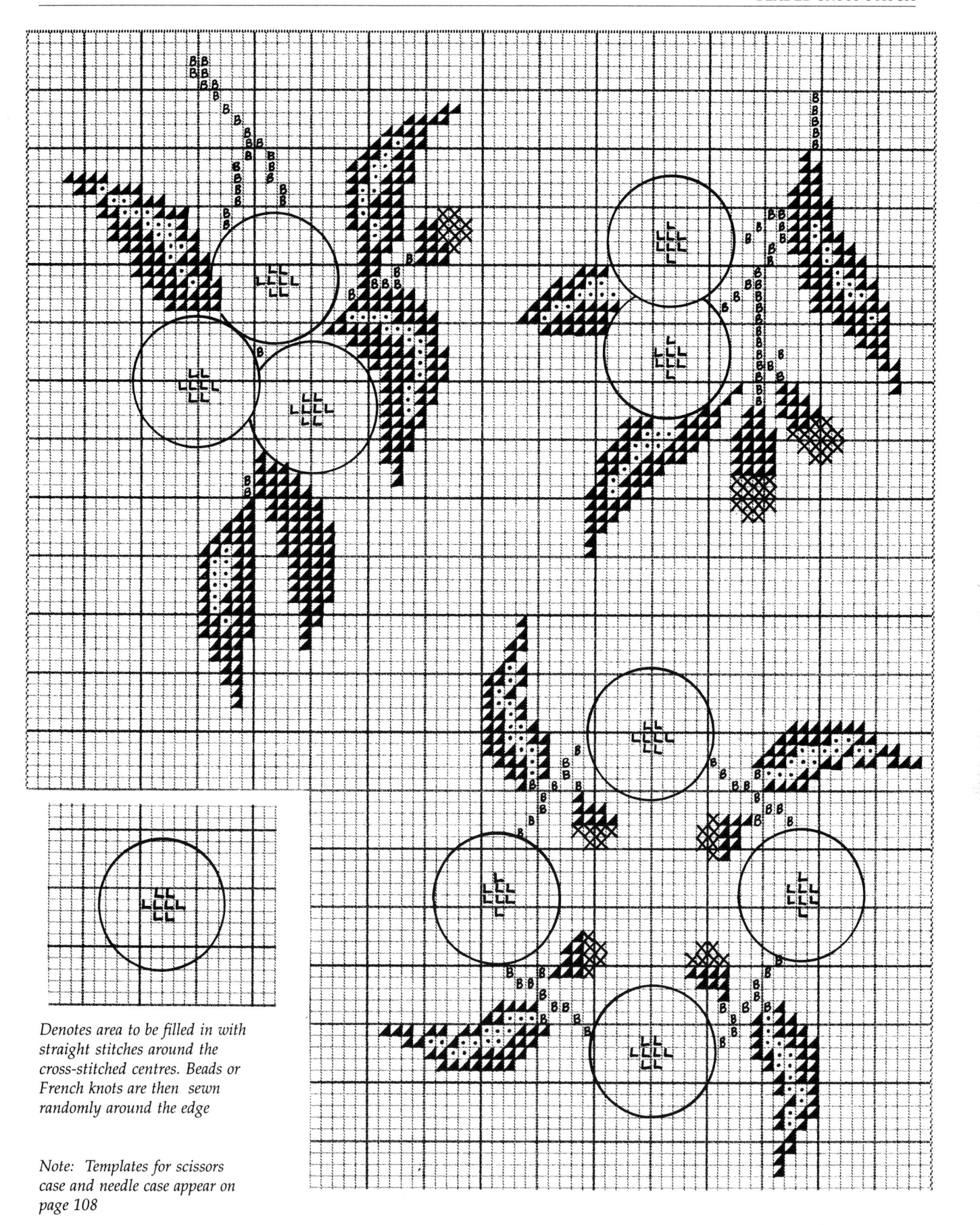

Denotes area to be filled in with straight stitches around the cross-stitched centres. Beads or French knots are then sewn randomly around the edge

Note: Templates for scissors case and needle case appear on page 108

51

Barrier Reef fishes picture embroidered in two strands of Minnamurra variegated threads onto 16 HPI Aida fabric painted with diluted fabric paints in green, aqua and pale lemon (graph on page 54)

Pillowcase border of bauera daisies worked onto a strip of Aida band using two strands of DMC variegated stranded cotton (graph on page 105)

SOURCEBOOK FOR AUSTRALIAN CROSS-STITCH

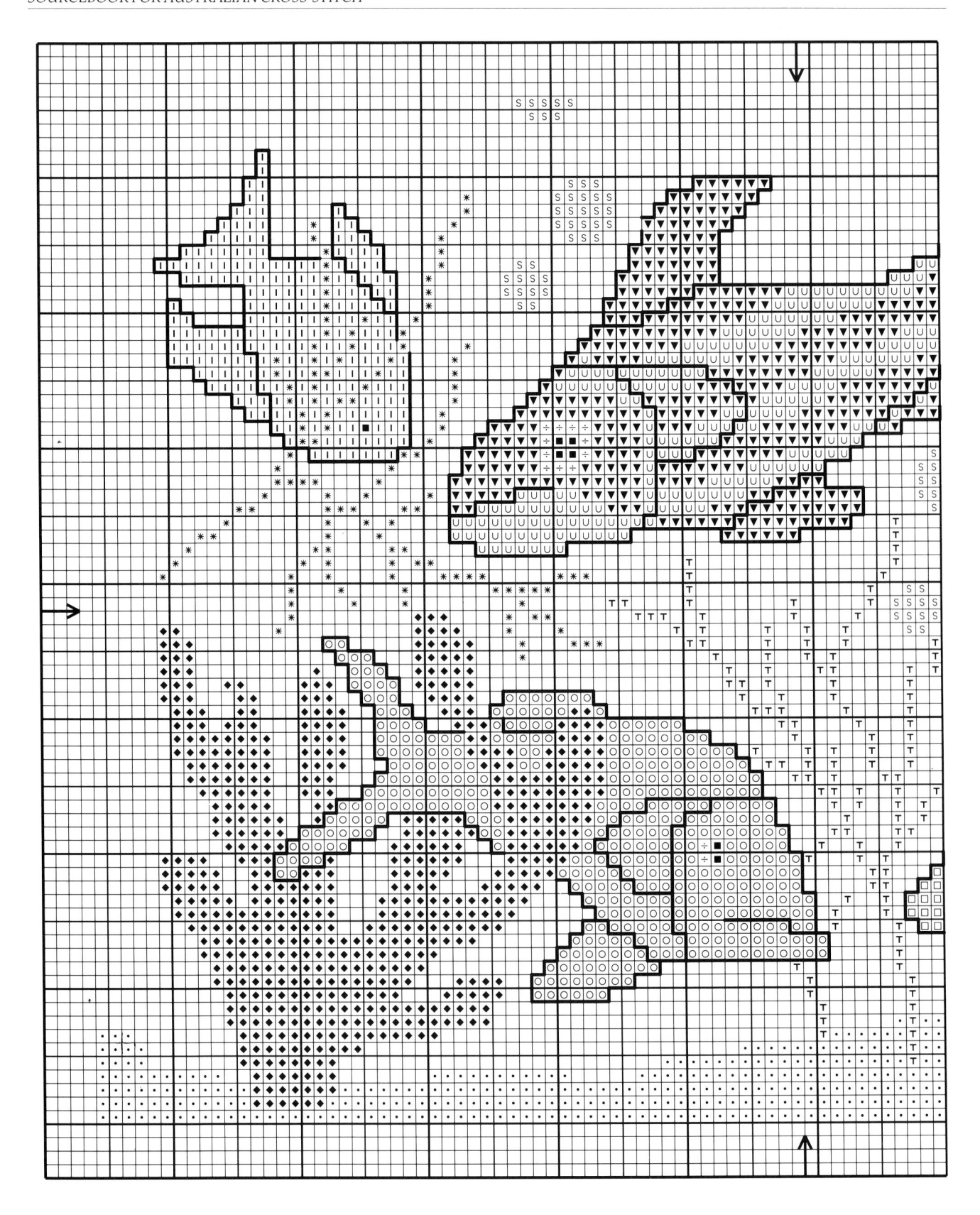

VARIEGATED THREADS

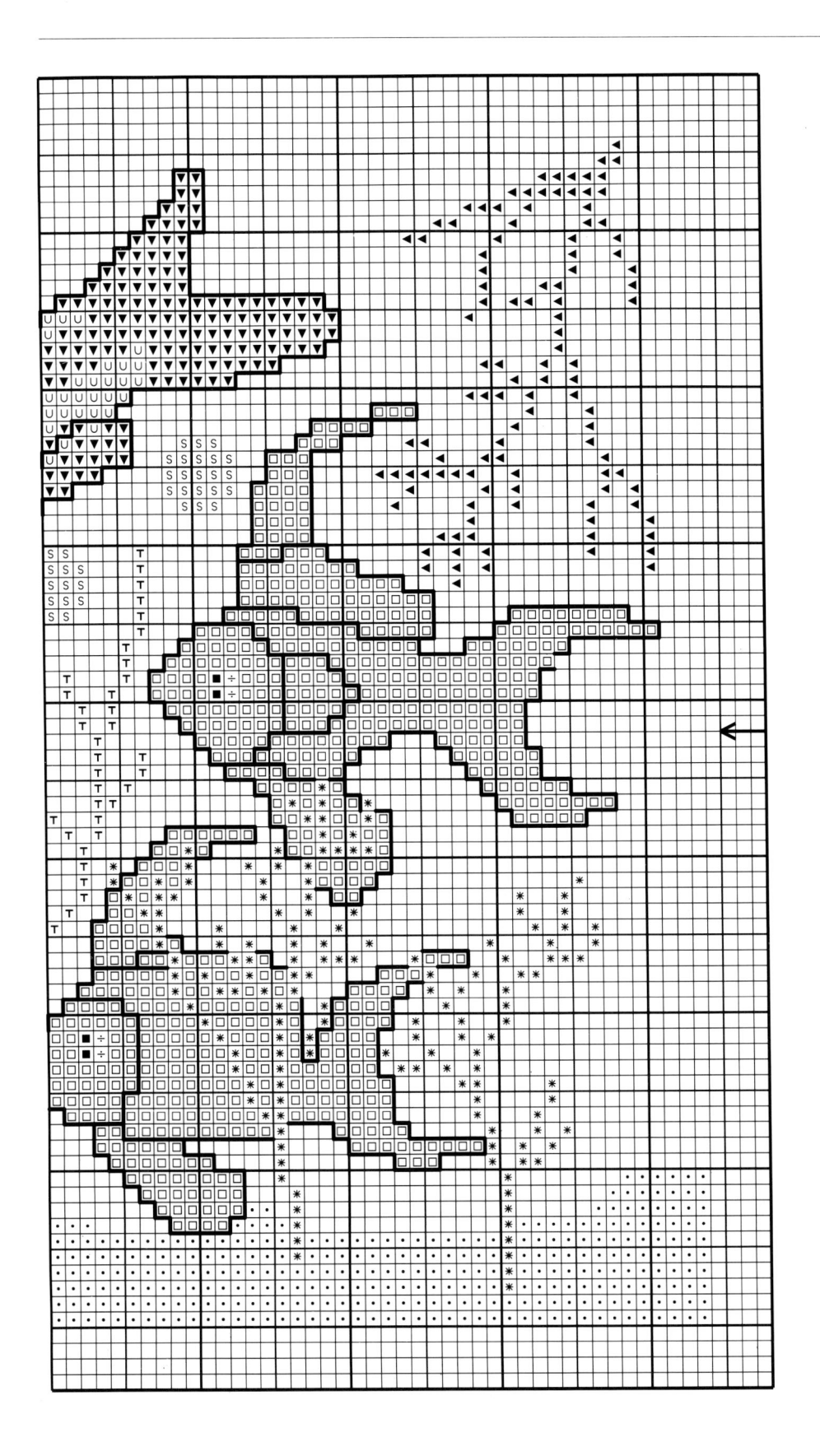

Barrier Reef Fish Key

Minnamurra Threads

◄	60	Blue/green/yellow
☐	30	Cerise/purple
T	250	Green
O	90	Red/blue
U	50	Apricot
S	190	Pink/blue
✶	180	Yellow/green
◆	70	Emerald/lime
I	170	Aqua/grey
▼	100	Orange
•	210	Olive/orange

DMC Threads

÷		ECRU Cream
■	3799	Charcoal
⌐	3799	Charcoal

55

SOURCEBOOK FOR AUSTRALIAN CROSS-STITCH

The lyrebird's body is worked in three strands of stranded cotton while its tail is stitched in Rajmahal metallic gold thread, on 14 HPI Aida cloth (graph appears on page 58)

METALLIC THREADS

Dragonfly is sewn onto 14 HPI Aida cloth using two strands of stranded cotton, while the wings are sewn in a double strand of pearl metallic thread (graph appears on page 106)

SOURCEBOOK FOR AUSTRALIAN CROSS-STITCH

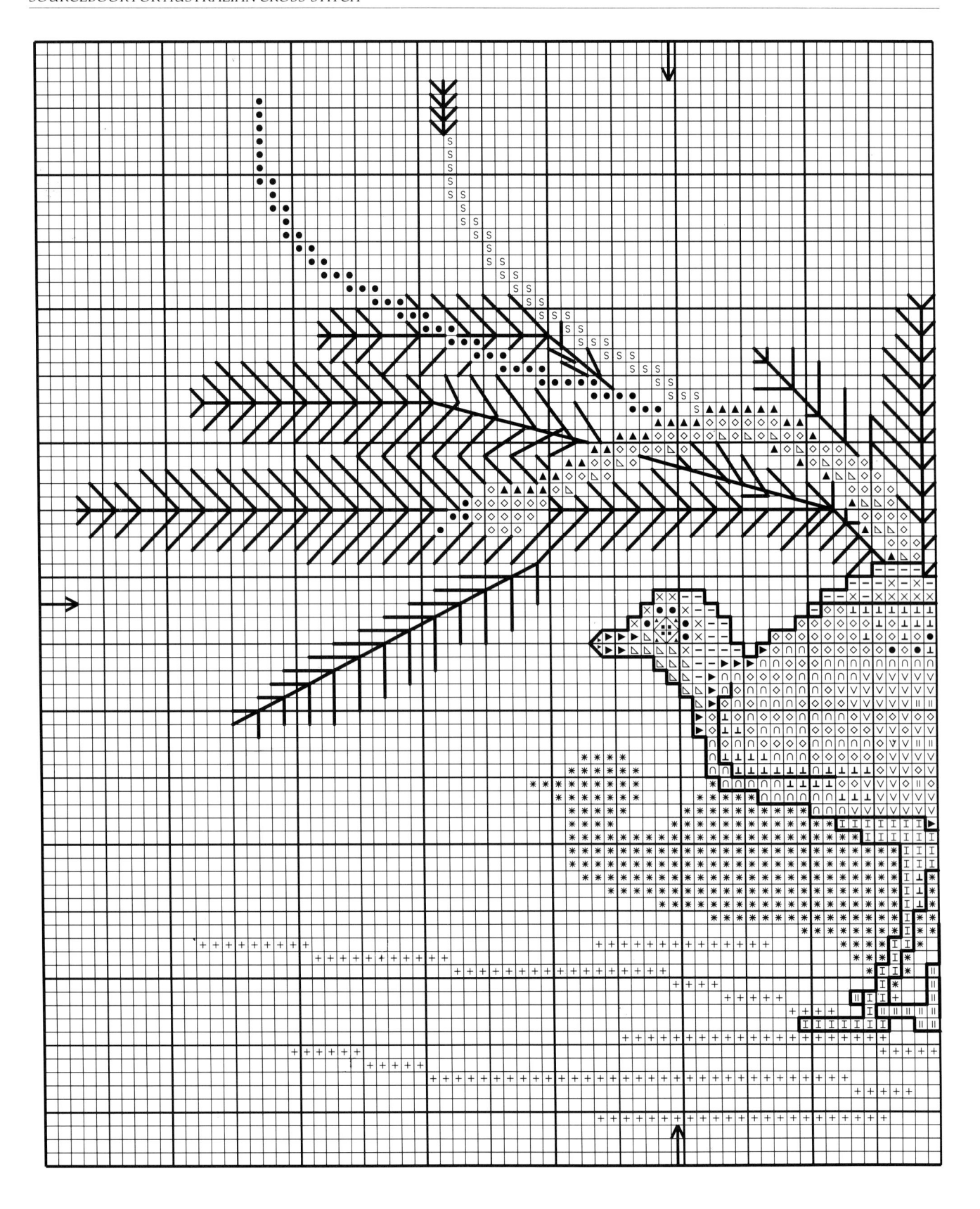

METALLIC THREADS

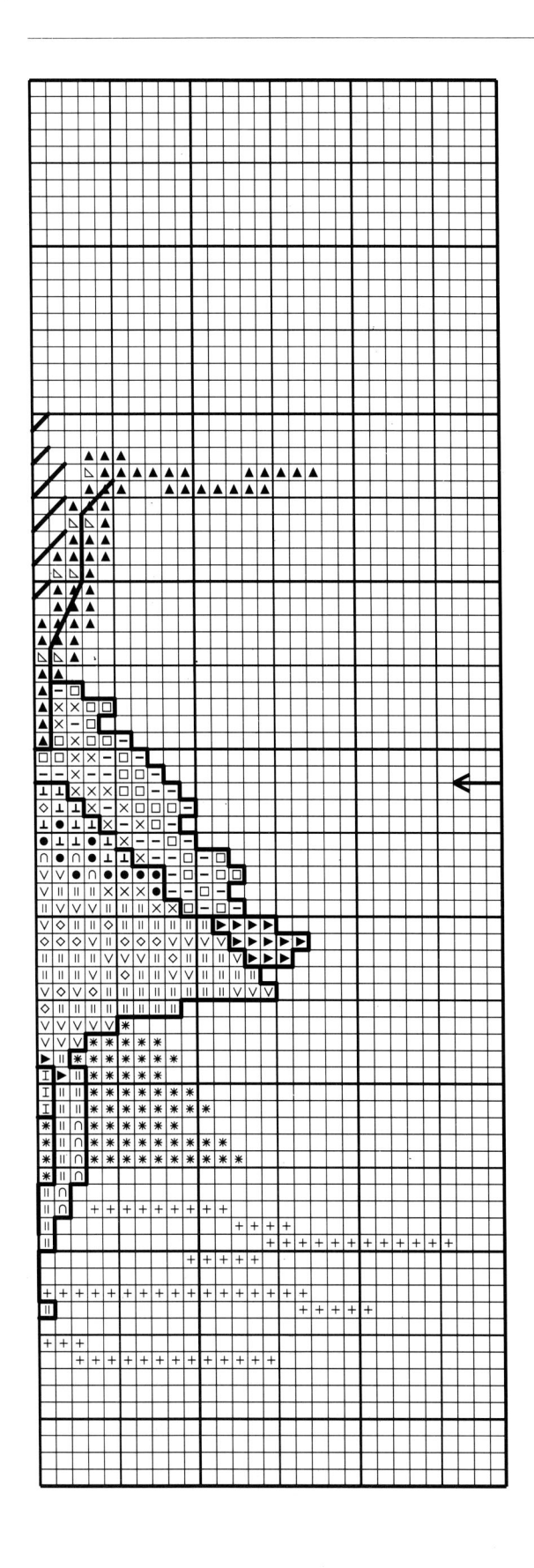

Lyrebird Key

DMC Threads

- ■ 310 Black
- ☒ 645 Dark Grey
- ⊟ 3022 Medium Grey
- ☐ 3023 Light Grey
- ▲ Ecru Cream
- ⊞ 782 Old Gold
- ✳ 3363 Green
- I 3047 Buff
- ‖ 301 Light Rust
- ∩ 3790 Mid Brown
- ● 3046 Beige
- ⊥ 841 Light Brown
- ▶ 938 Very Dark Brown
- ◺ 977 Orange
- V 918 Dark Rust
- ◇ 839 Dark Brown
- ⌐ 938 Brown Outline
- ⌐ 977 Tail Feather

Rajmahal Threads

- S Gold Handsew Thread
- ⌐ Gold Outline

59

SOURCEBOOK FOR AUSTRALIAN CROSS-STITCH

The wattle wreath dramatically demonstrates the different effects obtained when the same design is worked onto a self-patterned damask panel, on 16 HPI Aida cloth in a framed picture and onto silk gauze using a single strand of thread, all with DMC stranded thread

SILK GAUZE

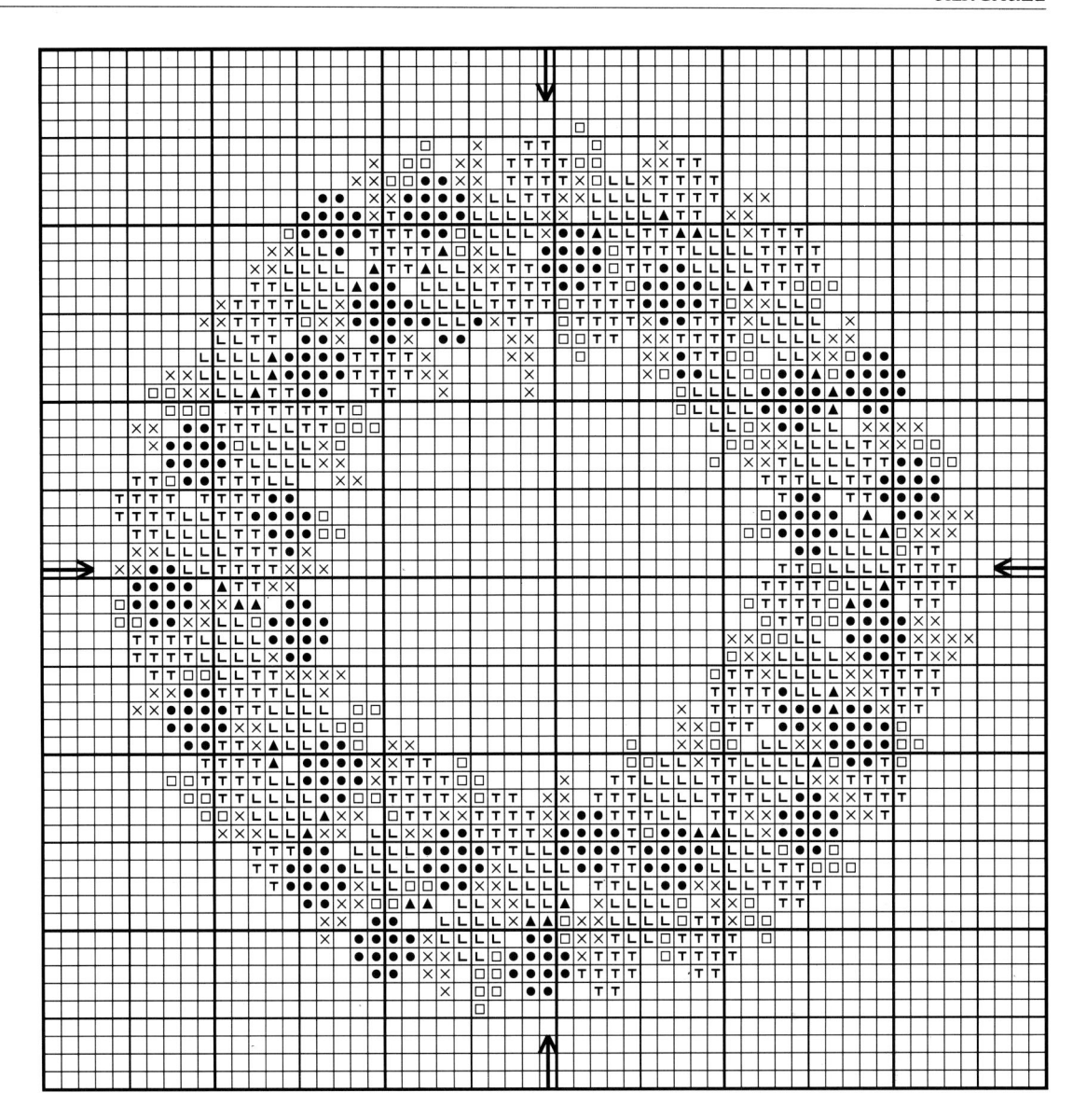

Wattle Wreath Key

DMC Stranded Cotton

- ● 972 Golden Yellow
- L 744 Pale Lemon
- T 743 Bright Yellow
- X 522 Leaf Green
- ▲ 840 Brown
- □ 3362 Dark Green

SOURCEBOOK FOR AUSTRALIAN CROSS-STITCH

Butterfly cloth corner border worked in three strands of stranded cotton on a table centre with pre-woven zig-zag border panel, readily available from craft shops

BORDERS

SOURCEBOOK FOR AUSTRALIAN CROSS-STITCH

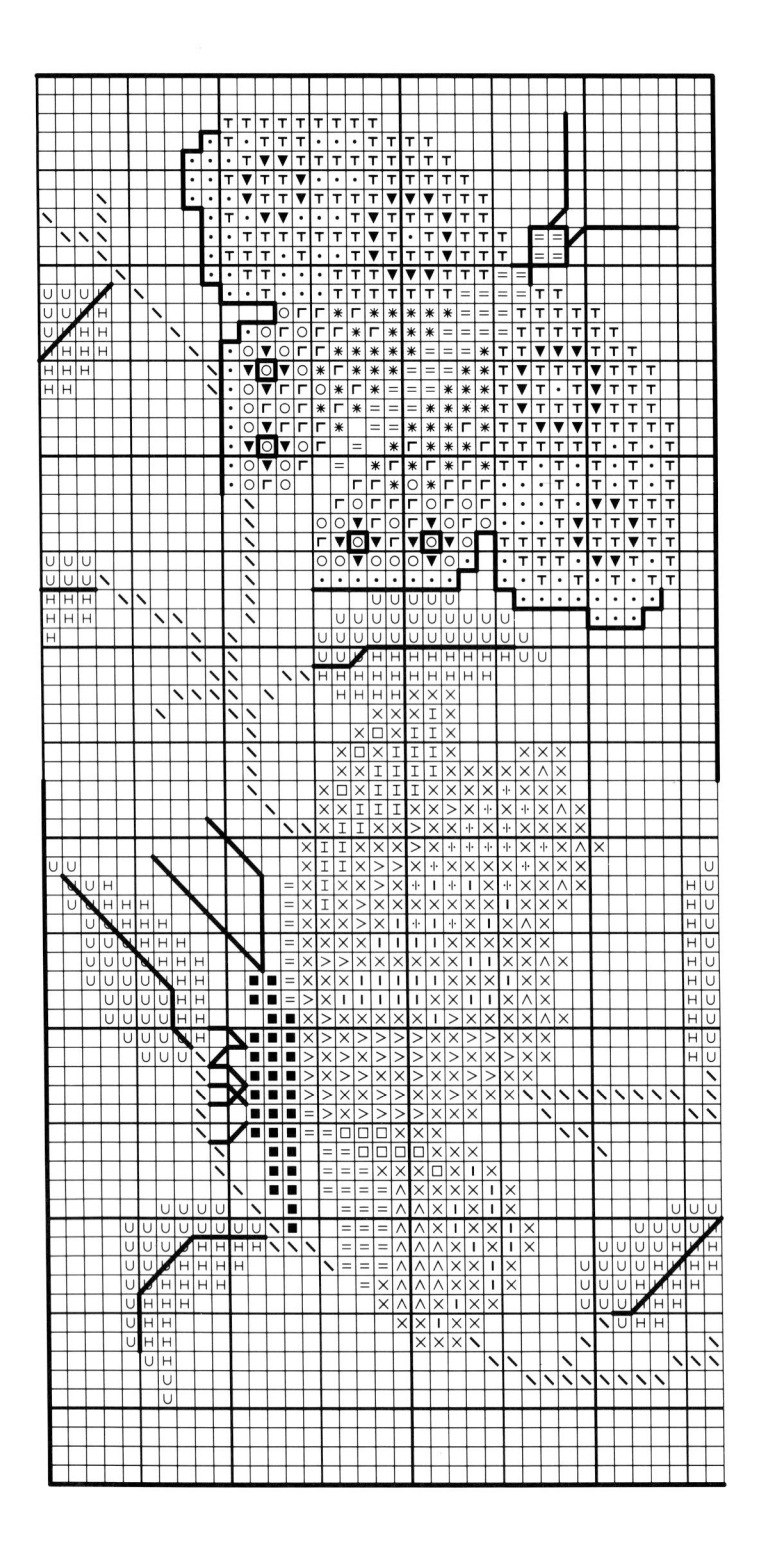

BORDERS

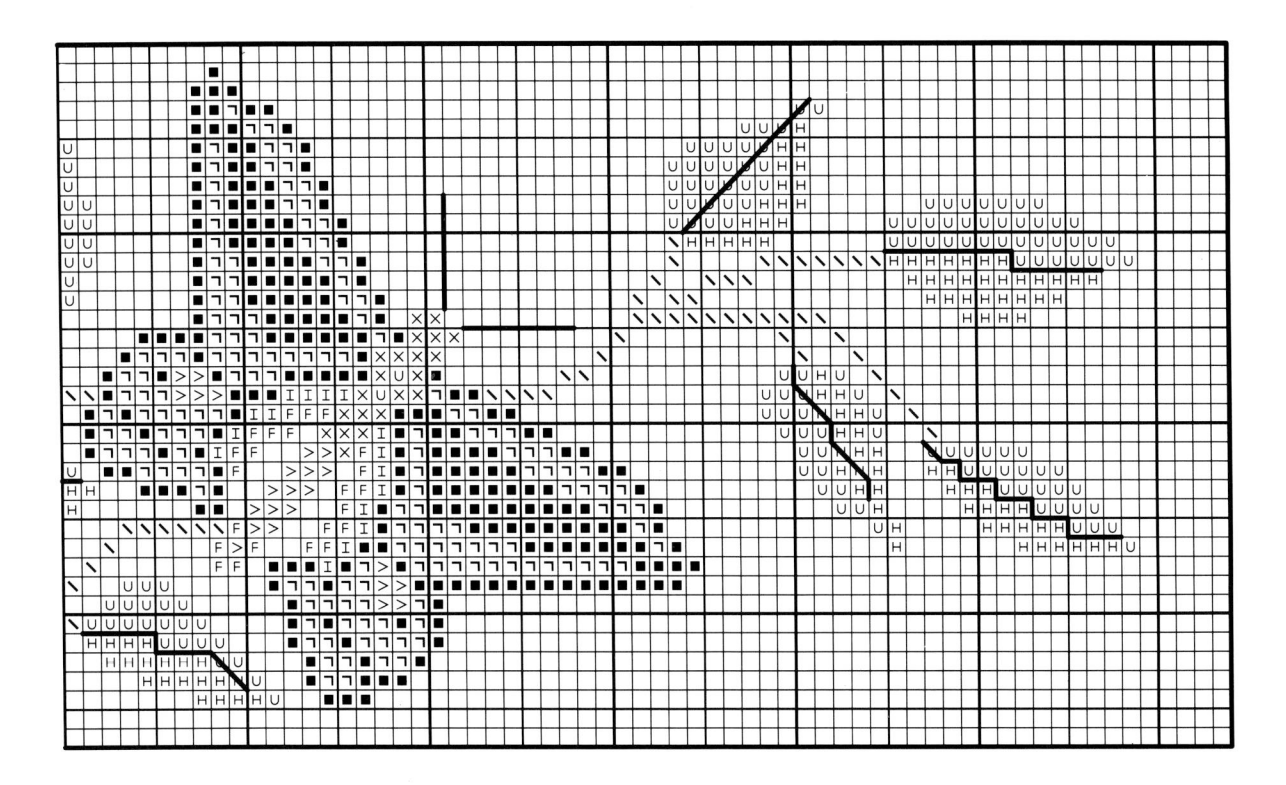

Butterfly Cloth Key

DMC Threads

■	310	Black	←	996	Aqua Blue
X	839	Dark Brown	N	995	Turquoise
>	725	Yellow	S	646	Gunmetal Grey
ø	971	Bright Orange	F	841	Taupe
⊡	900	Terracotta	I	3774	Pale Taupe
Z	721	Burnt Orange	\	632	Rust Brown
▽	722	Pale Orange	H	731	Dark Green
·	Blanc	White	U	733	Light Green
T	413	Charcoal	⌐	905	Emerald Green
✳	797	Dark Blue	·|·	727	Pale Yellow
⌐	798	Mid Blue	◻	3047	Deep Cream
O	799	Light Blue	I	726	Yellow
▼	3064	Fawn	∧	972	Golden Yellow
=	840	Brown	⌐	922	Leaf Veins
+	3072	Silver grey	⌐	310	Black Antennae

SOURCEBOOK FOR AUSTRALIAN CROSS-STITCH

Penguins sewn onto a pre-woven towelling baby's bib using two strands of stranded cotton. If you wish you can work a simplified version as a multi-penguin border strip without the grasses

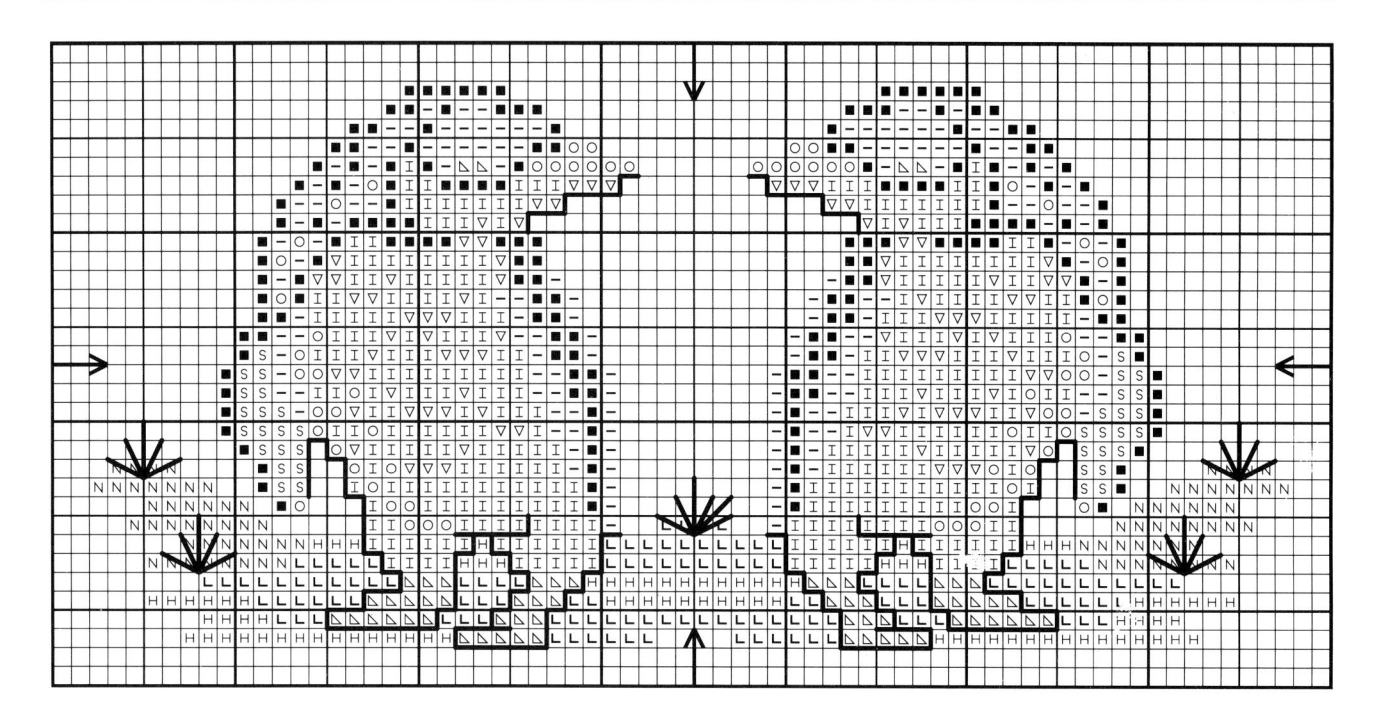

BORDERS

Baby Penguin Key

DMC Stranded Cotton

■	310	Black	◿	976	Gold
−	844	Dark Grey	N	524	Light Green
O	646	Light Grey	L	522	Mid Green
▽	842	Fawn	H	520	Dark Green
S	3770	Apricot	⌐	520	Grass Dark Green
I	Blanc White		⌐	310	Outline on Penguin

67

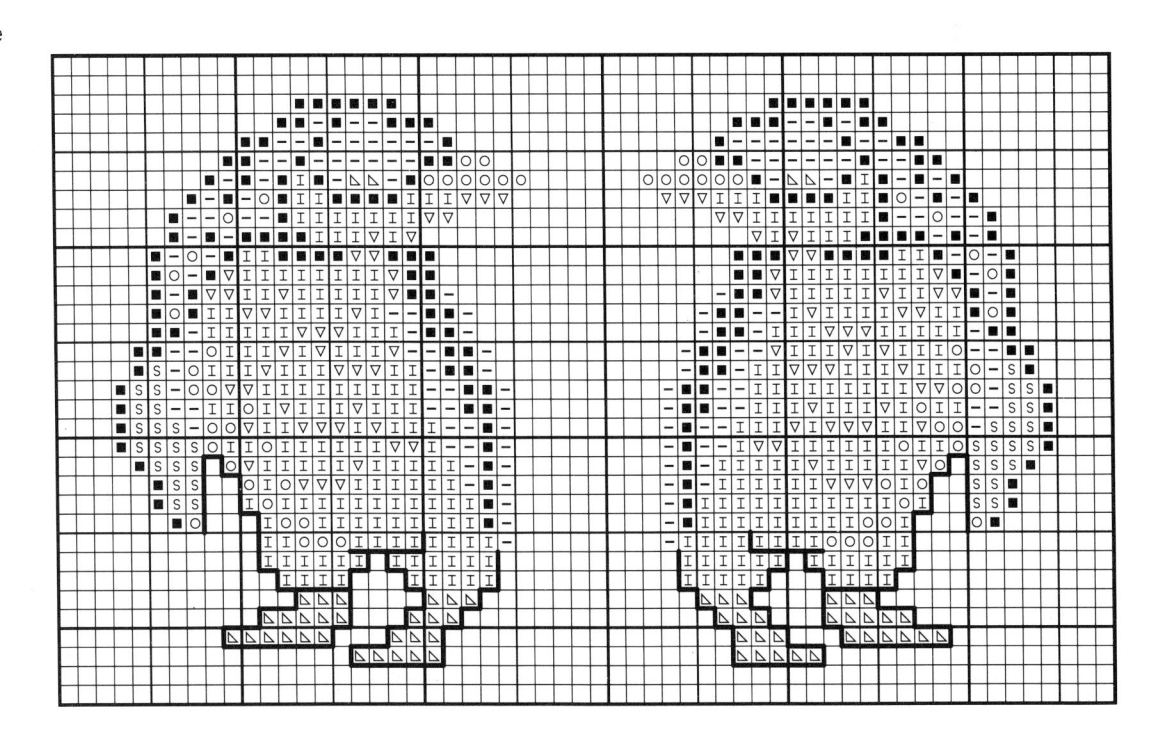

SOURCEBOOK FOR AUSTRALIAN CROSS-STITCH

Butterfly border worked in three strands of stranded cotton onto a towel with a pre-woven border strip; the Sturt's desert pea border is worked onto a strip of Aida band using two strands of stranded cotton (graph on page 70)

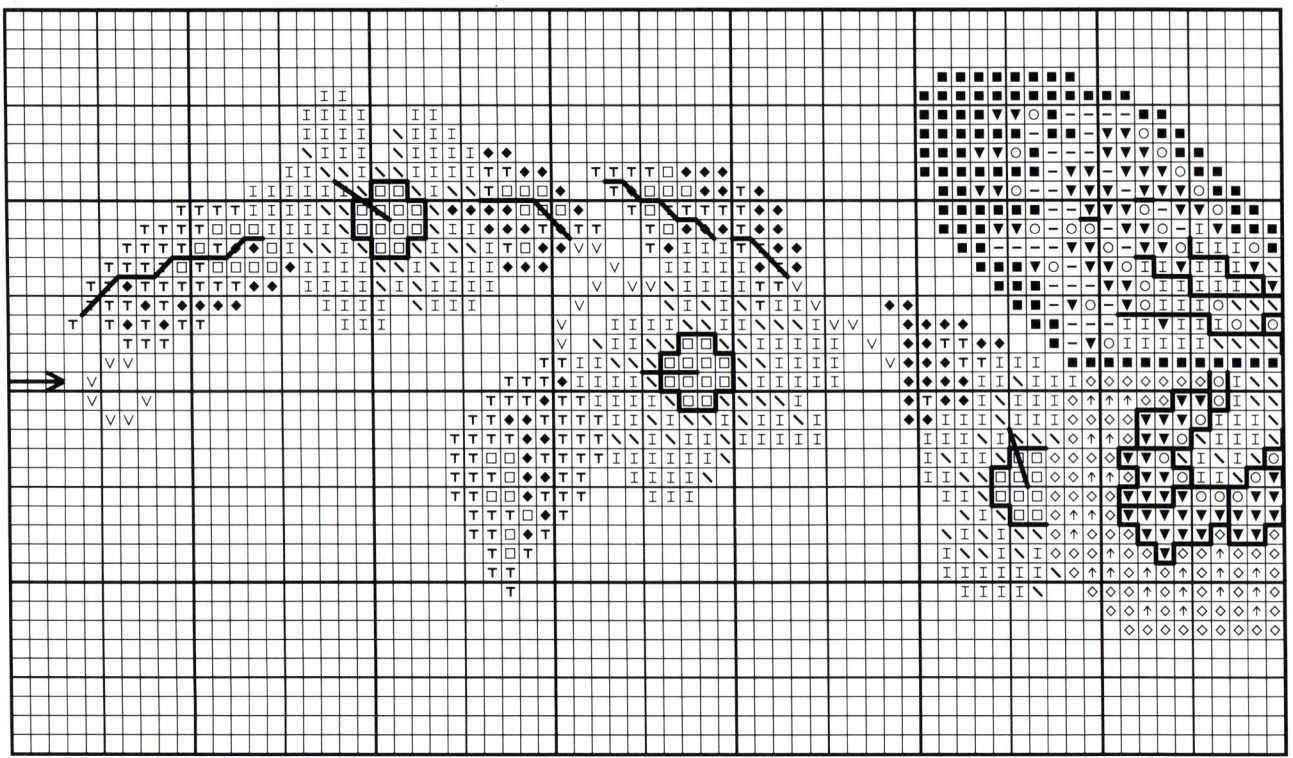

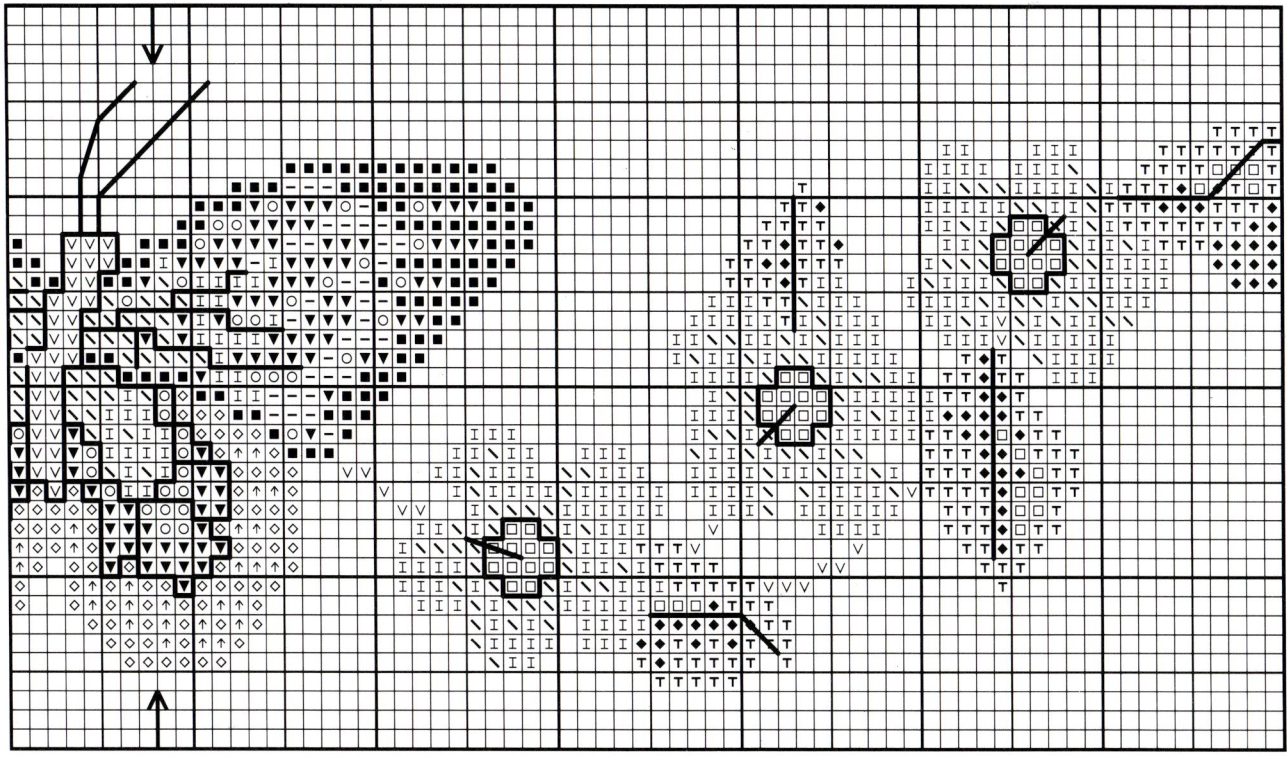

BORDERS

69

Sturt Pea Key

DMC Threads

- ■ 310 Black
- U 815 Maroon
- = 321 Dark Red
- ↑ 666 Bright Red
- ▲ 3772 Brown
- ✱ 3051 Dark Green
- Z 522 Medium Green
- H 524 Light Green

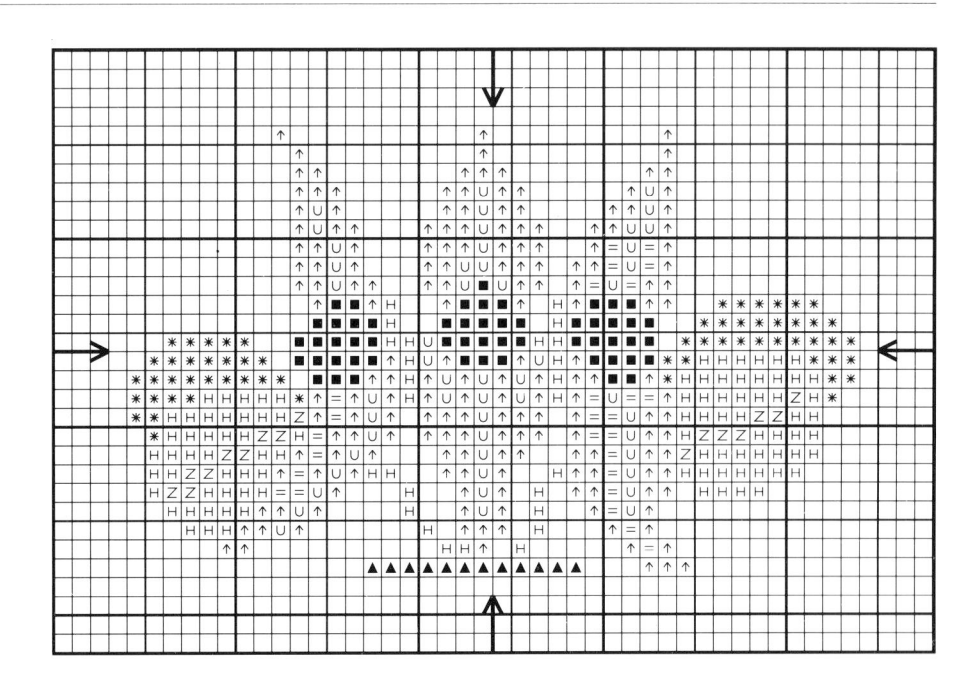

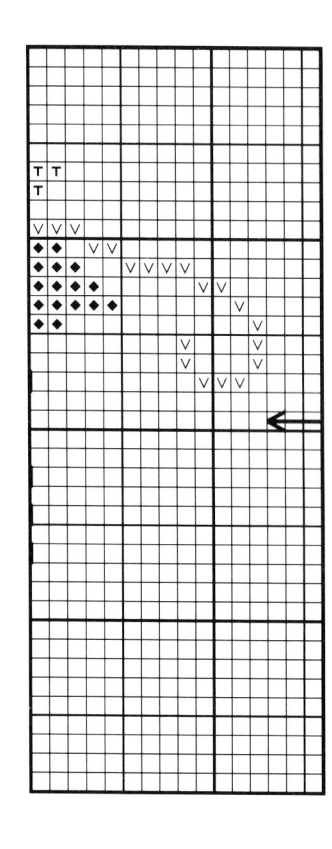

Butterfly Border Key

DMC Stranded Cotton

- ■ 310 Black
- − 317 Charcoal
- O 3752 Deep Blue
- ▼ 3753 Light Blue
- \ 726 Gold
- I 3078 Yellow
- ◆ 3346 Dark Green
- T 581 Olive Green
- □ 772 Light Green
- V 3772 Rust
- ◇ 839 Brown
- ↑ 666 Red
- ⌐ 310 Black

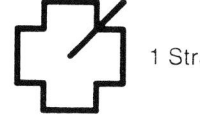

1 Strand 3772

PAINTED BACKGROUNDS

The silhouettes of the grass trees are worked in one, two and three strands of stranded cotton on bright yellow 14 HPI Aida cloth which has been painted with fabric paints, graduating from purple at the top to red and orange at the bottom

Key   DMC Stranded Cotton

- ■ 310 Black 3 Strands
- | 310 Black 2 Strands Backstitch
- ↓ 310 Black 1 Strand Straight Stitch
- ∨ 310 Black 1 and 2 Strand Straight Stitch
- ∧∧ 310 Black 2 Strands Straight Stitch
- ✳ 310 Black 1 Strand Straight Stitch

71

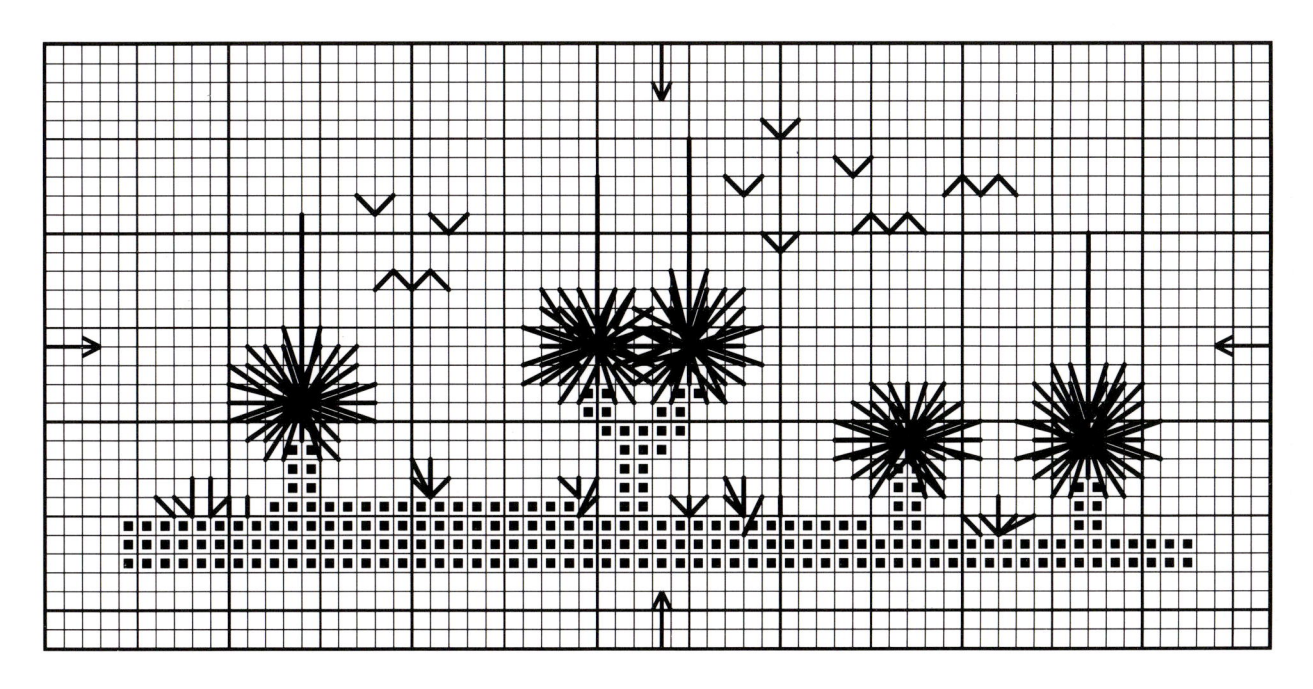

SOURCEBOOK FOR AUSTRALIAN CROSS-STITCH

The silhouette of the Murray River willow is embroidered in the same manner as the grass trees on painted 14 HPI Aida cloth

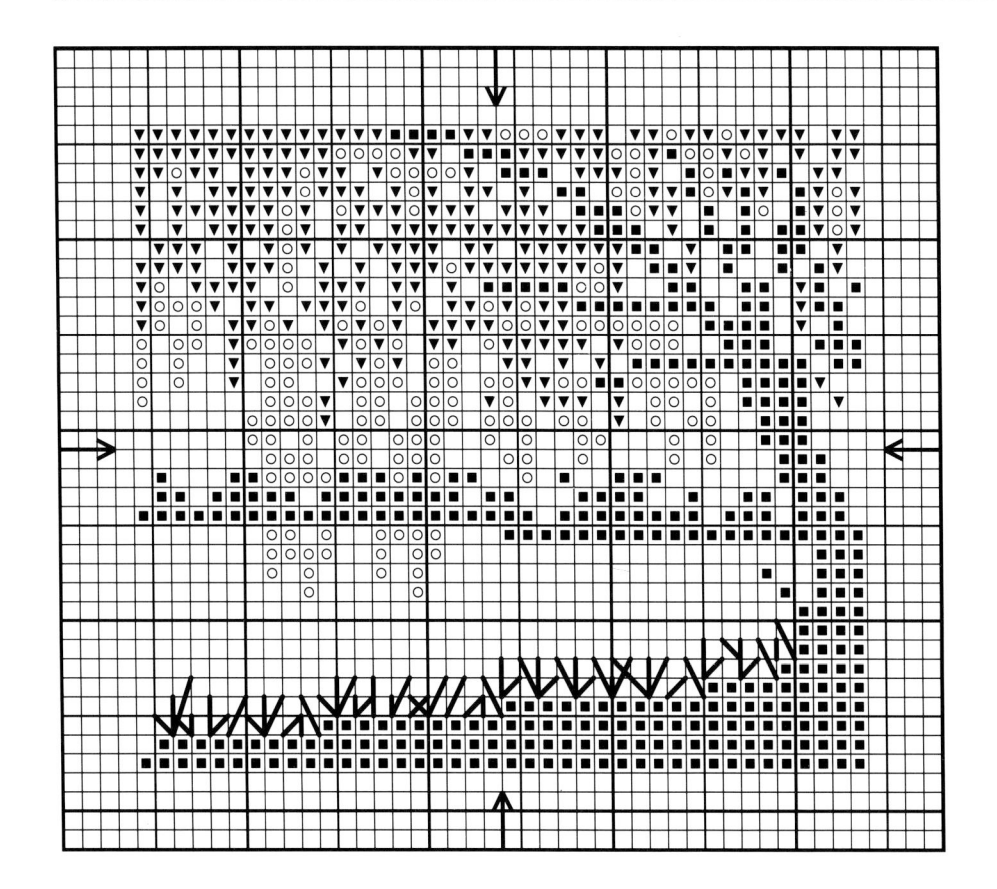

Murray River Willow Silhouette Key

DMC Stranded Cotton

- ◯ 310 Black 1 Strand
- ▼ 310 Black 2 Strands
- ■ 310 Black 3 Strands
- ⌐ 310 Black Straight Stitches

SOURCEBOOK FOR AUSTRALIAN CROSS-STITCH

The frill-necked lizard is worked in two strands of stranded cotton on 14 HPI Aida cloth which has been painted with diluted folk art paints, graduating from blue at the top to orange and light green at the bottom

PAINTED BACKGROUNDS

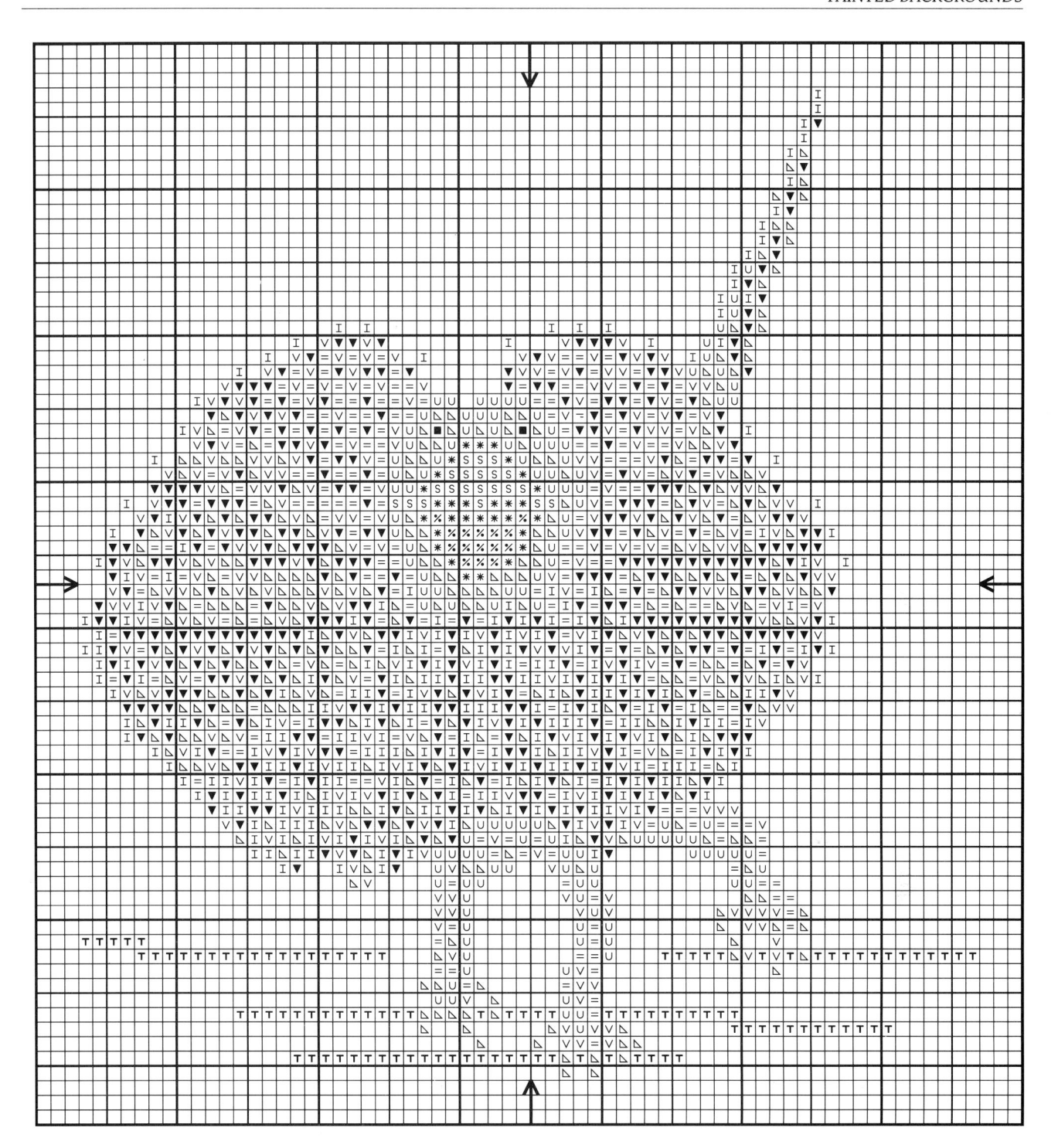

Frill-necked Lizard Key

DMC Stranded Cotton

- ■ 310 Black
- U 3777 Maroon
- = 3830 Burgundy
- % 666 Red
- ✱ 352 Deep Pink
- S 754 Light Pink
- T 3053 Dull Green
- I 3827 Pale Gold
- ◺ 721 Orange
- V 356 Rust
- ▼ 433 Brown

75

SOURCEBOOK FOR AUSTRALIAN CROSS-STITCH

DESIGN PORTFOLIO

Echidna embroidered onto 16 HPI Aida fabric using two strands of stranded cotton (graph on page 107)

OPPOSITE: *Waratah design worked in three strands of stranded cotton onto a 14 HPI Aida woven cushion panel with coloured trim (graph on page 78)*

SOURCEBOOK FOR AUSTRALIAN CROSS-STITCH

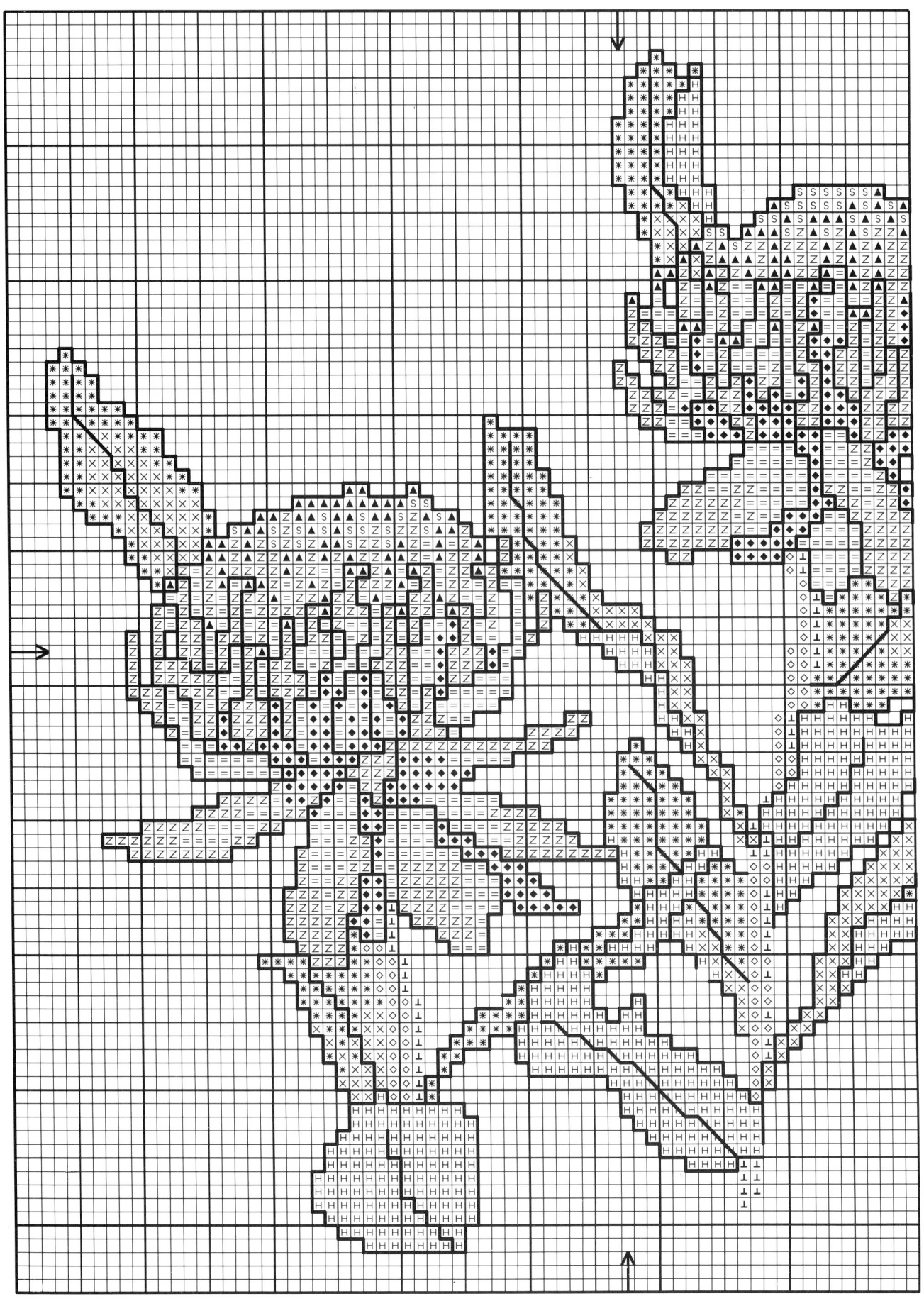

DESIGN PORTFOLIO

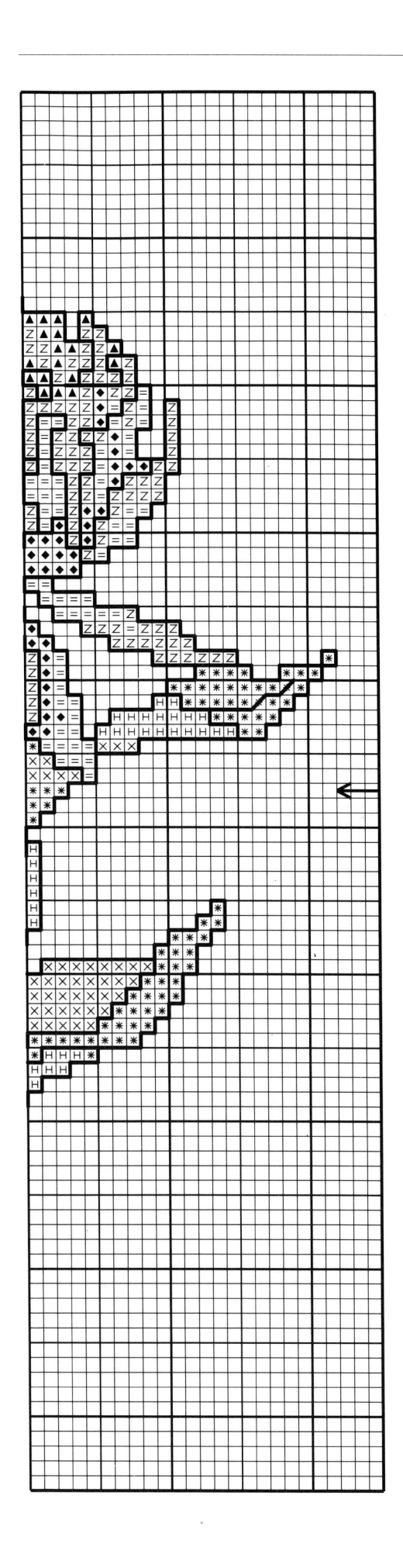

Waratah Key

DMC Threads

☒	319	Very dark Green
☐	304	Medium Red
▲	351	Deep Orange
Ⓢ	353	Light Orange
✳	986	Dark Green
Ⓩ	666	Bright Red
Ⓗ	320	Light Green
◆	815	Dark Red
⊥	610	Dark Brown
◇	371	Light Brown
⌐	902	Outline Flowers
⌐	610	Leaf Veins
⌐	726	Outline Leaves

Yellow-breasted robins sewn onto 16 HPI Aida fabric using two strands of stranded cotton

DESIGN PORTFOLIO

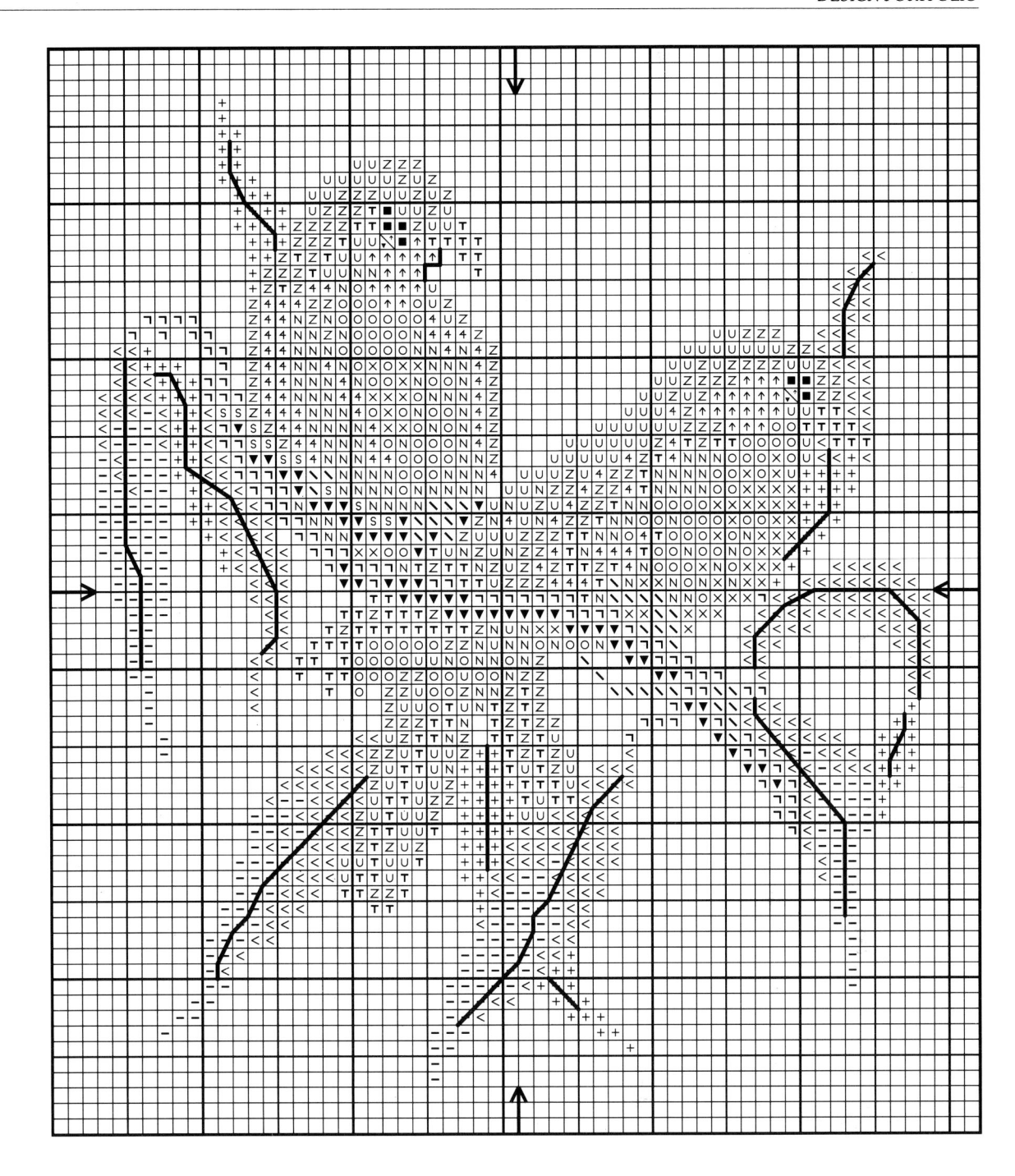

Yellow-Breasted Robin Key

DMC Threads

- ■ 310 Black
- T 844 Charcoal Grey
- Z 318 Medium Grey
- U 762 Silver Grey
- ↑ Blanc White
- 4 372 Khaki
- N 783 Mustard
- X 972 Orange
- O 726 Yellow
- S 950 Beige
- \ 919 Rust
- ⌐ 301 Brown
- − 503 Light Green
- < 502 Mid Green
- + 500 Dark Green
- ▼ 433 Dark Brown
- ⌐ 977 Leaf Veins
- ⌐ 310 Black Bird Outline

81

SOURCEBOOK FOR AUSTRALIAN CROSS-STITCH

Penguin on a rock, sewn in three strands of stranded cotton with the water worked in half crosses, using a single strand of thread on 14 HPI Aida cloth

DESIGN PORTFOLIO

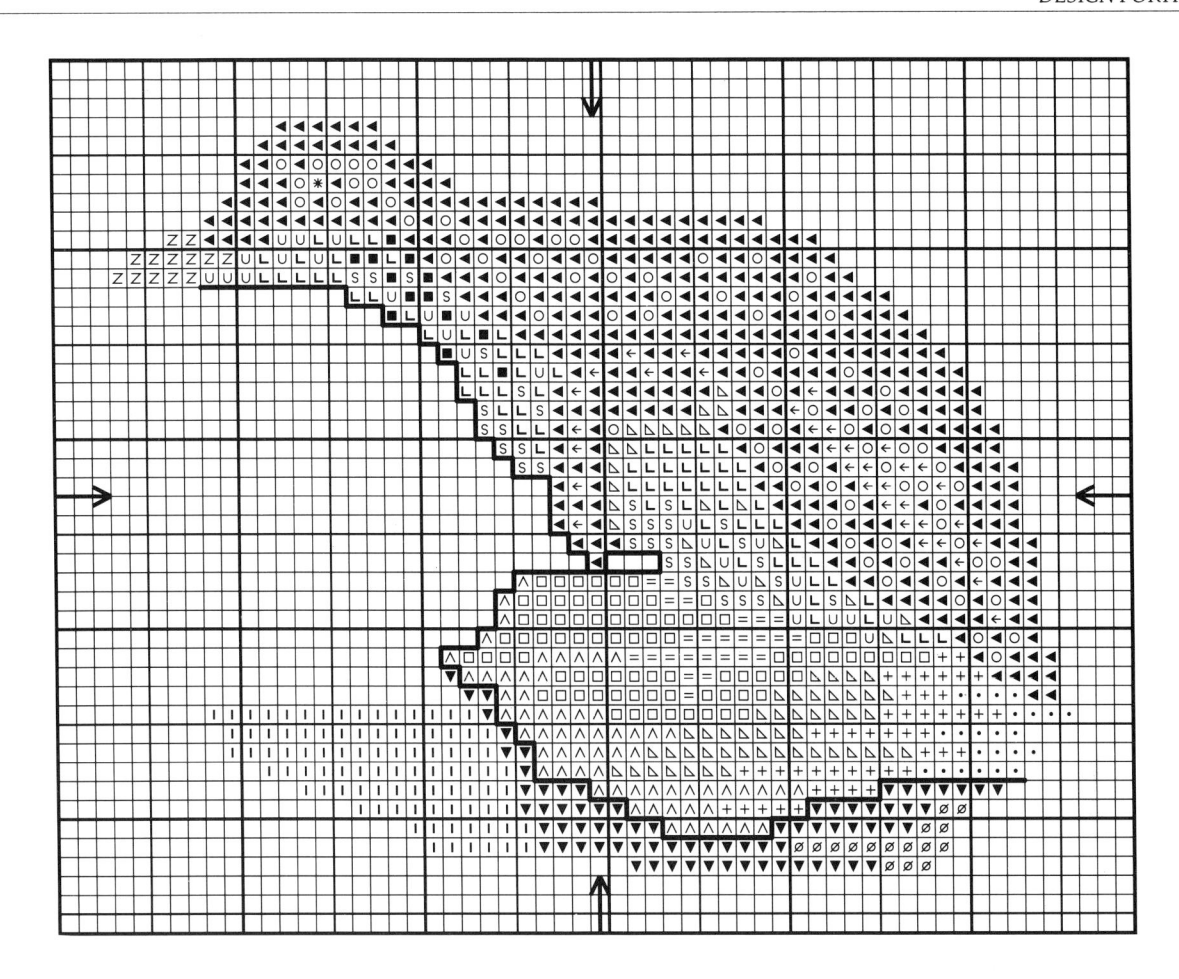

Penguin Key

DMC Threads

- ■ 647 Grey
- ○ 824
- + 3348 Green
- U 3072 Silver Grey
- = 436 Burnt Orange
- S 739 Dark Orange
- ✱ 744 Pale Lemon
- L Blanc White
- Z 646 Gunmetal Grey
- ▫ Ecru Cream
- I 3766 Blue
- ▼ 3772 Rust
- ← 794
- ∧ 453
- ◀ 310 Black
- · 772 Pale Orange
- ⌀ 898 Blue
- ◺ 738 Green
- L 647 Grey

SOURCEBOOK FOR AUSTRALIAN CROSS-STITCH

Pink fairy basslets worked in two strands of stranded cotton on the woven band of a terry-towelling handtowel

DESIGN PORTFOLIO

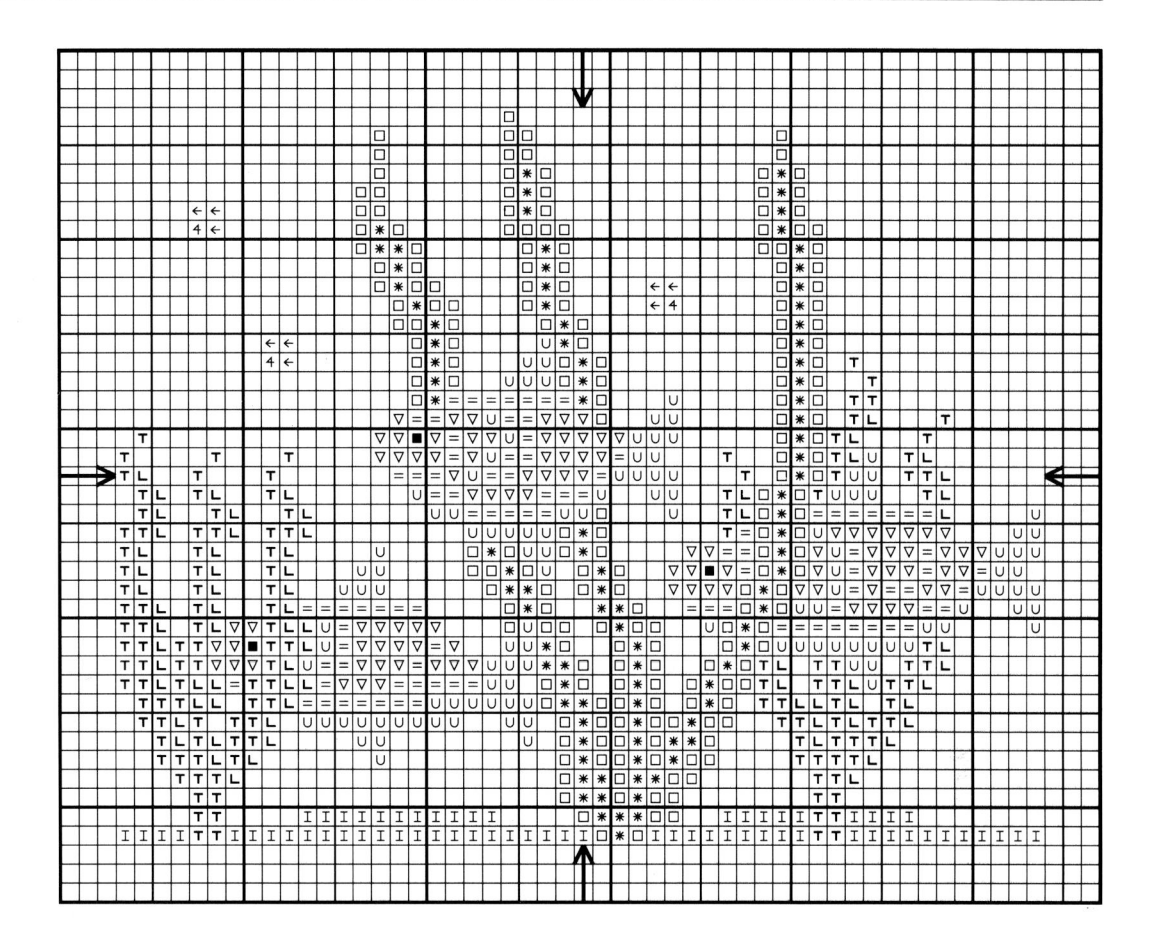

Pink Fairy Basslets Key

DMC Threads

- [4] 598 Aqua
- [←] 747 Pale Aqua
- [□] 320 Light Green
- [*] 895 Dark Green
- [■] 310 Black
- [L] 730 Dark Olive Green
- [T] 733 Light Olive Green
- [U] 347 Red
- [=] 956 Bright Pink
- [∇] 3713 Pale Pink
- [I] 677 Cream

Kookaburra sewn in three strands of stranded cotton onto a background of 14 HPI Aida cloth

DESIGN PORTFOLIO

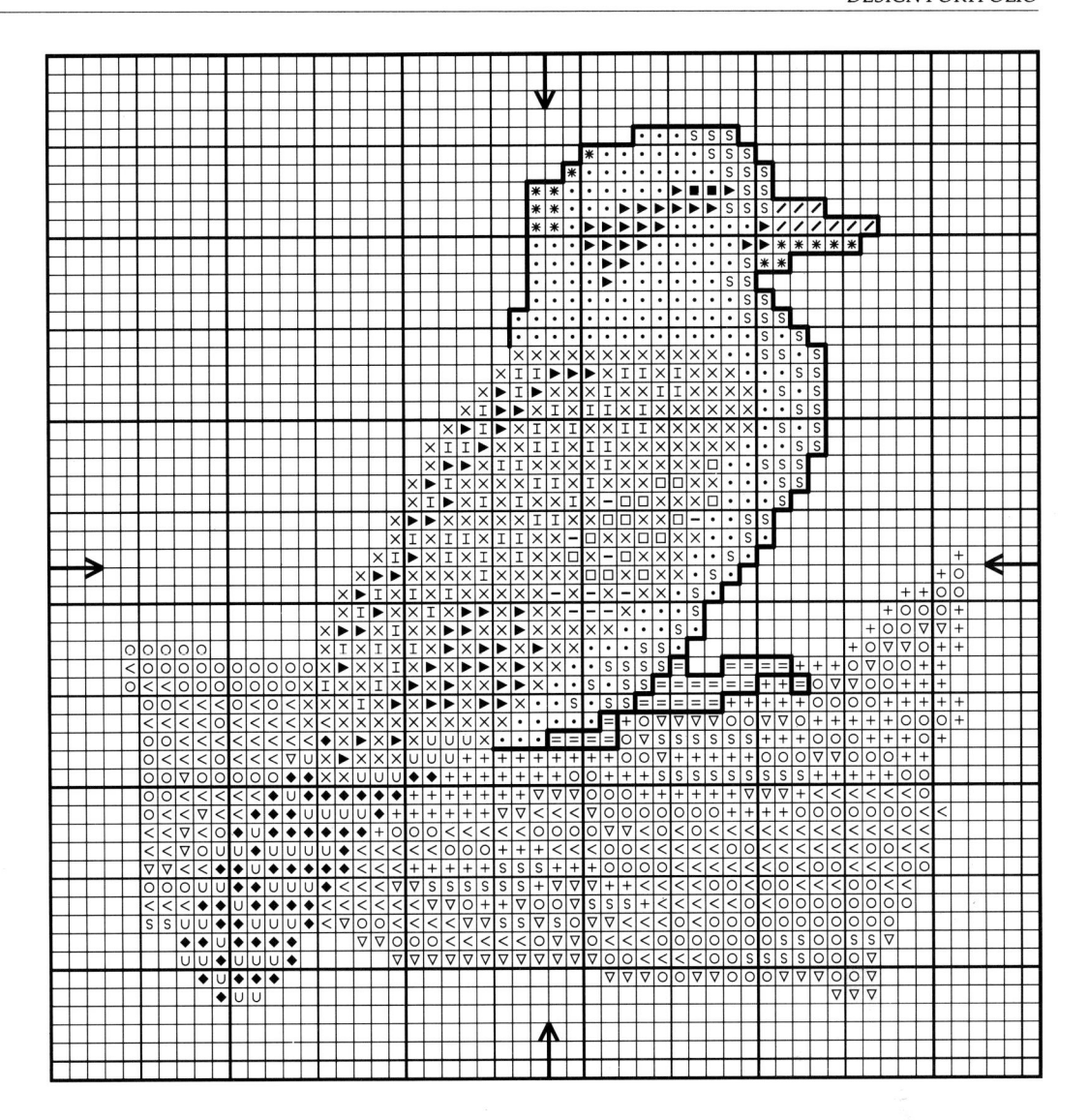

Kookaburra Key

DMC Stranded Cotton

- ■ 310 Black
- · Ecru Cream
- − 518 Dark Blue
- O 415 Light Grey
- + 3022 Dark Grey
- = 3045 Light Brown
- ▽ 3772 Rust
- S 613 Fawn Chest
- < 3033 Deep Cream
- I 612 Camel
- ◆ 838 Chocolate Brown
- □ 519 Light Blue
- U 436 Burnt Orange
- ▶ 3790 Taupe
- ∕ 414 Grey Beak
- X 310/3790 1 strand of each
- ✳ 3770 Apricot
- ⌈ 3790 Outline

SOURCEBOOK FOR AUSTRALIAN CROSS-STITCH

Ulysses butterfly picture worked in two strands of stranded cotton over two threads of Belfast linen

88

DESIGN PORTFOLIO

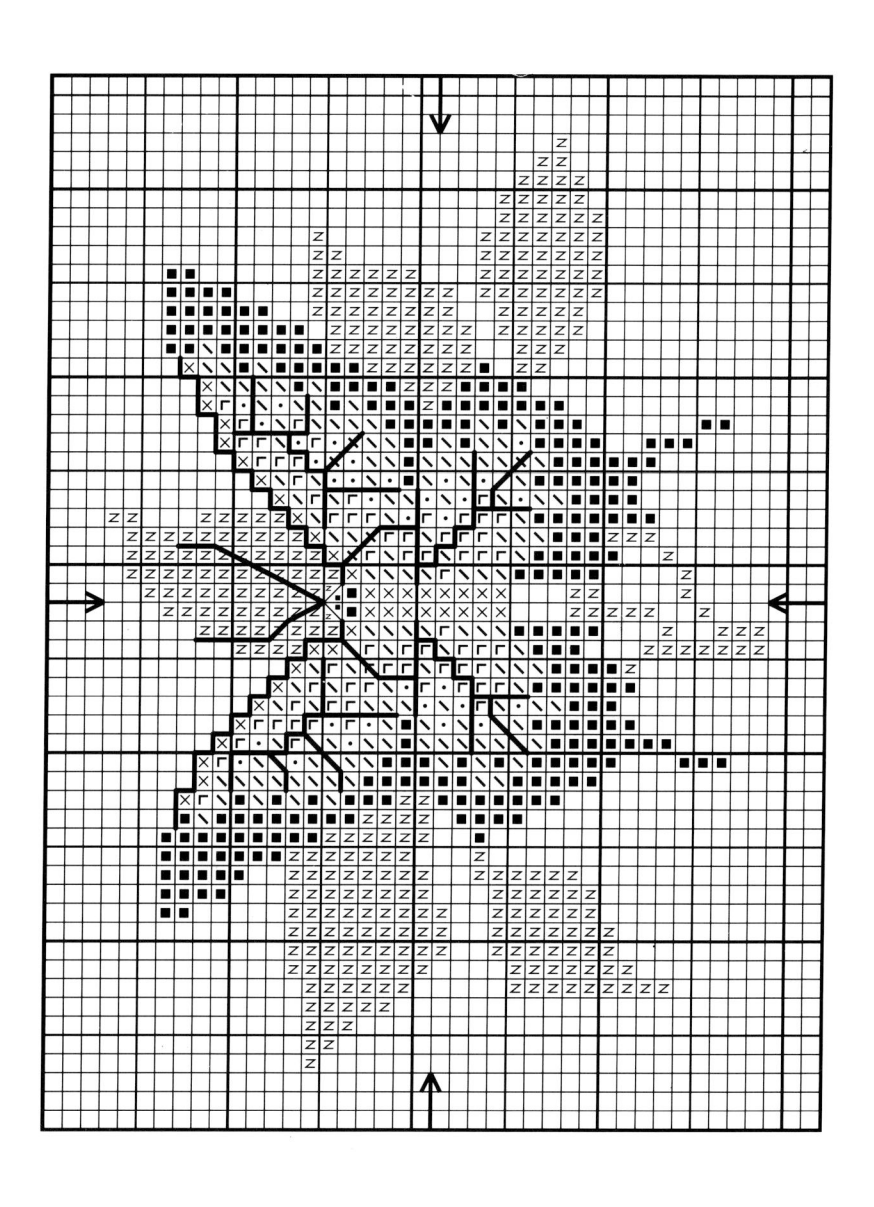

Ulysses Butterfly Key

DMC Stranded Cotton

- ■ 310 Black
- ╲ 995 Turquoise
- ⌐ 996 Aqua
- ✗ 930 Dark Blue
- • 3746 Purple
- Z 3053 Green
- ⌐ 310 Black Outline

89

Marsupial mice sewn onto a background of 16 HPI Aida cloth using two strands of stranded cotton

DESIGN PORTFOLIO

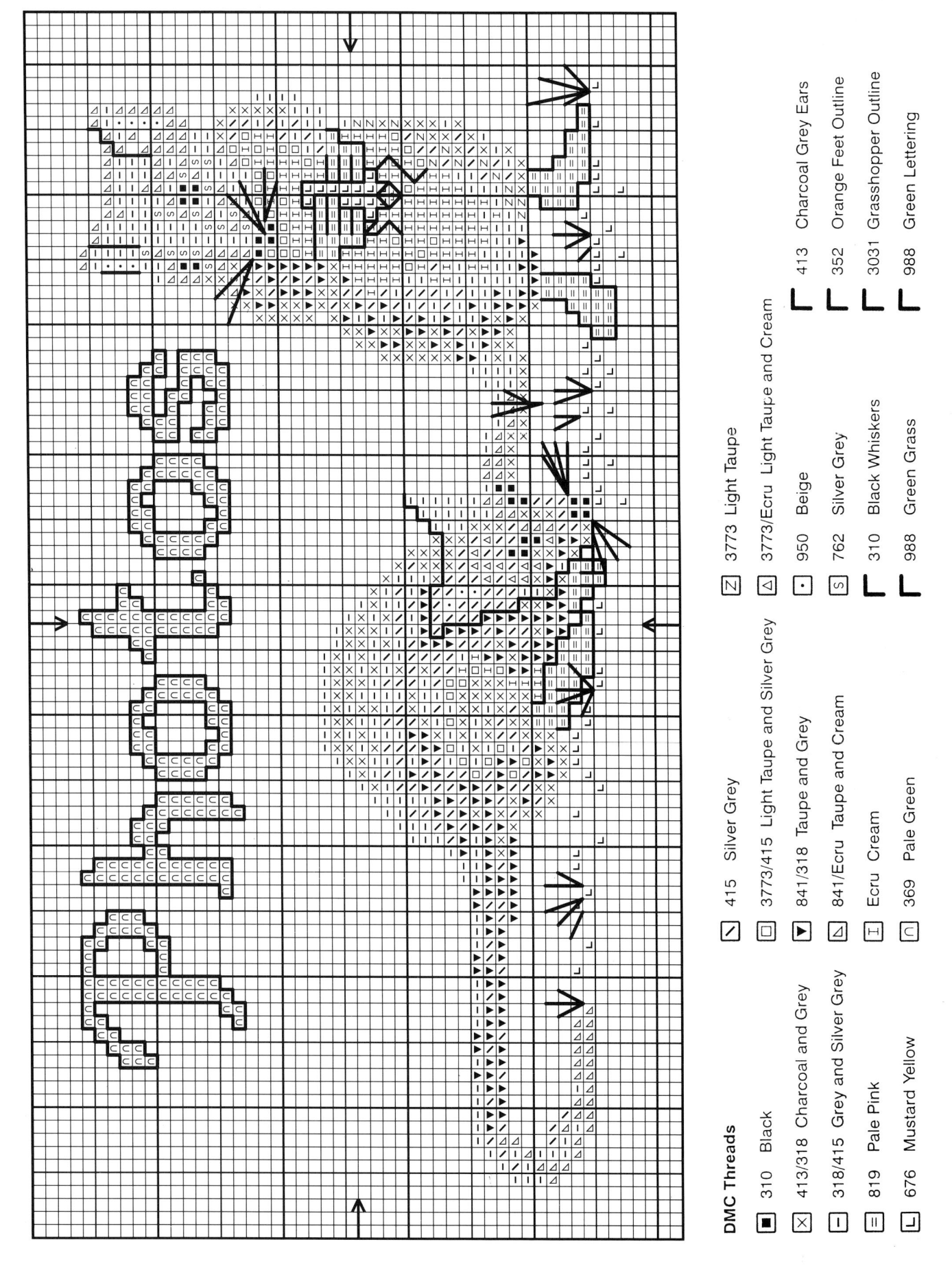

DMC Threads

Symbol	Code	Description
■	310	Black
X	413/318	Charcoal and Grey
I	318/415	Grey and Silver Grey
=	819	Pale Pink
L	676	Mustard Yellow

Symbol	Code	Description
/	415	Silver Grey
□	3773/415	Light Taupe and Silver Grey
▶	841/318	Taupe and Grey
△	841/Ecru	Taupe and Cream
H	Ecru	Cream
C	369	Pale Green

Symbol	Code	Description
Z	3773	Light Taupe
⋈	3773/Ecru	Light Taupe and Cream
•	950	Beige
S	762	Silver Grey
	310	Black Whiskers
L	988	Green Grass

Code	Description
413	Charcoal Grey Ears
352	Orange Feet Outline
3031	Grasshopper Outline
988	Green Lettering

91

New Holland honeyeater sewn onto a traycloth of 16 HPI Aida cloth using two strands of stranded cotton

DESIGN PORTFOLIO

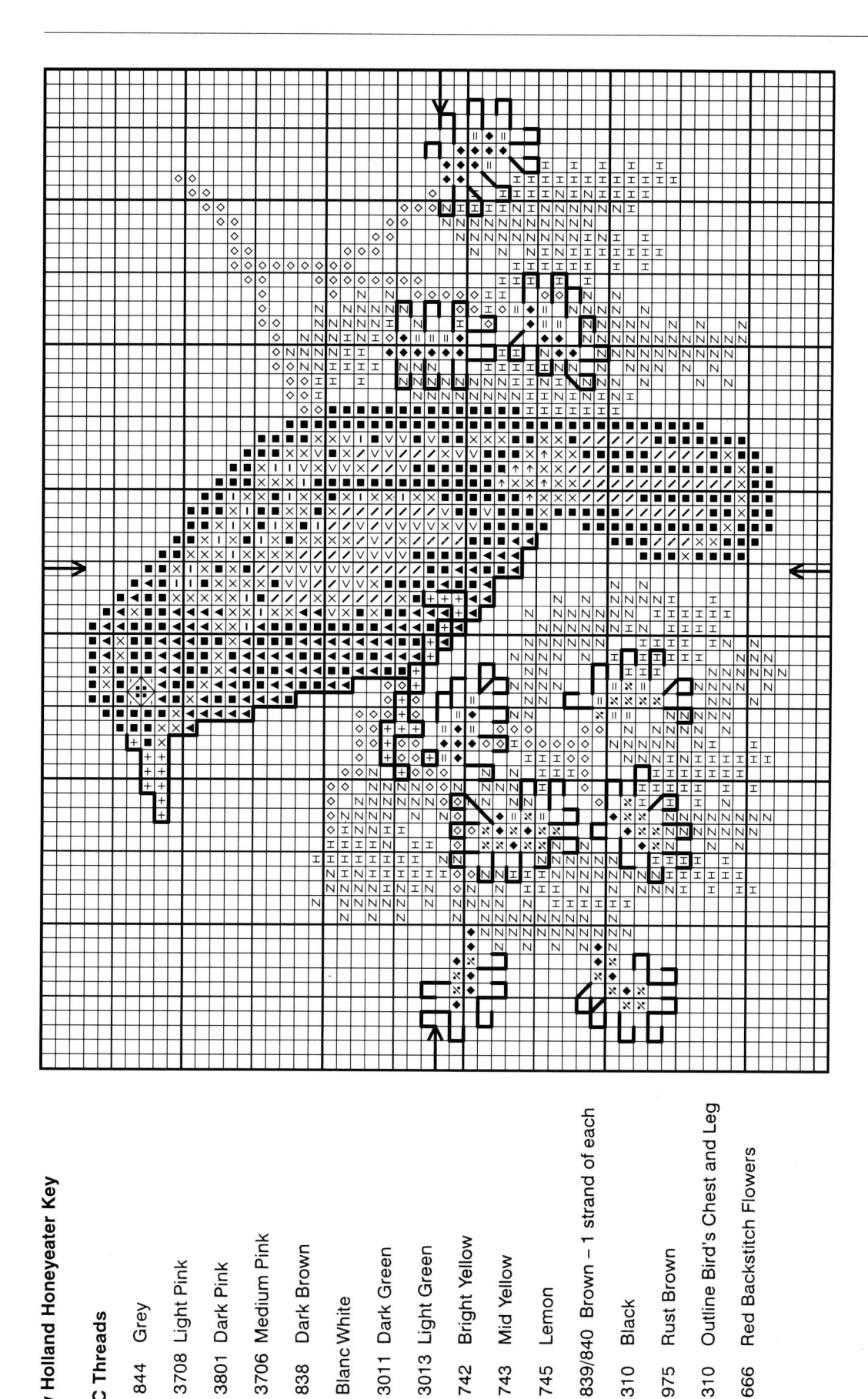

New Holland Honeyeater Key

DMC Threads

Symbol	Code	Colour
+	844	Grey
※	3708	Light Pink
=	3801	Dark Pink
◆	3706	Medium Pink
X	838	Dark Brown
◀	Blanc	White
N	3011	Dark Green
I	3013	Light Green
/	742	Bright Yellow
V	743	Mid Yellow
↑	745	Lemon
I	839/840	Brown – 1 strand of each
■	310	Black
◇	975	Rust Brown
L	310	Outline Bird's Chest and Leg
L	666	Red Backstitch Flowers

93

SOURCEBOOK FOR AUSTRALIAN CROSS-STITCH

The cottage is worked in two strands of stranded cotton onto grey-blue 14 HPI Aida cloth

DESIGN PORTFOLIO

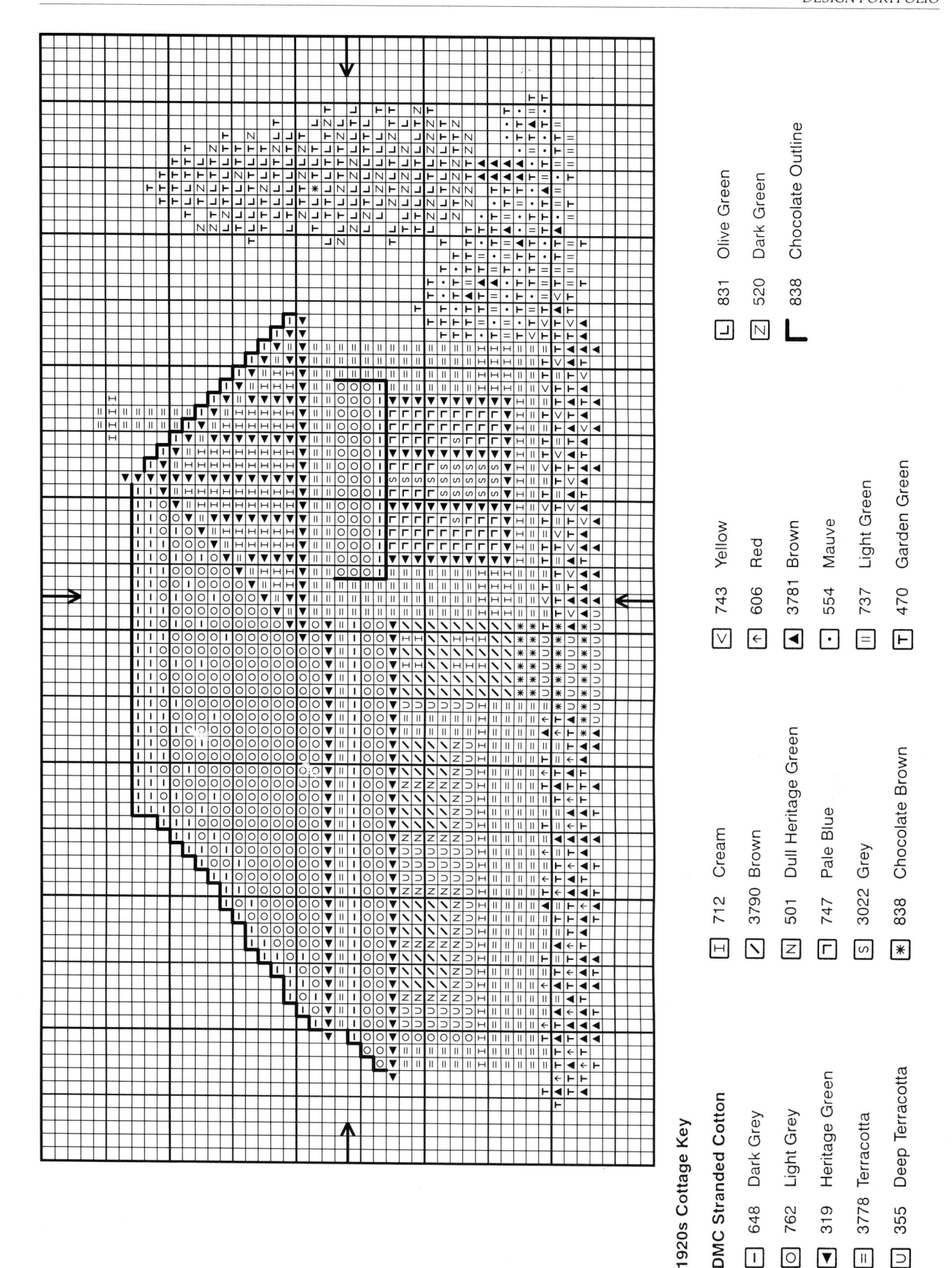

1920s Cottage Key
DMC Stranded Cotton

I	712	Cream	V	743	Yellow
O	648	Dark Grey	←	606	Red
▼	762	Light Grey	◀	3781	Brown
=	319	Heritage Green	·	554	Mauve
U	3778	Terracotta	=	737	Light Green
	355	Deep Terracotta	T	470	Garden Green
H	712	Cream	L	831	Olive Green
╲	3790	Brown	Z	520	Dark Green
N	501	Dull Heritage Green	⌐	838	Chocolate Outline
⌐	747	Pale Blue			
S	3022	Grey			
✶	838	Chocolate Brown			

95

SOURCEBOOK FOR AUSTRALIAN CROSS-STITCH

The dolphins disporting themselves across the beach bag are sewn onto 14 HPI Aida fabric with three strands of stranded cotton

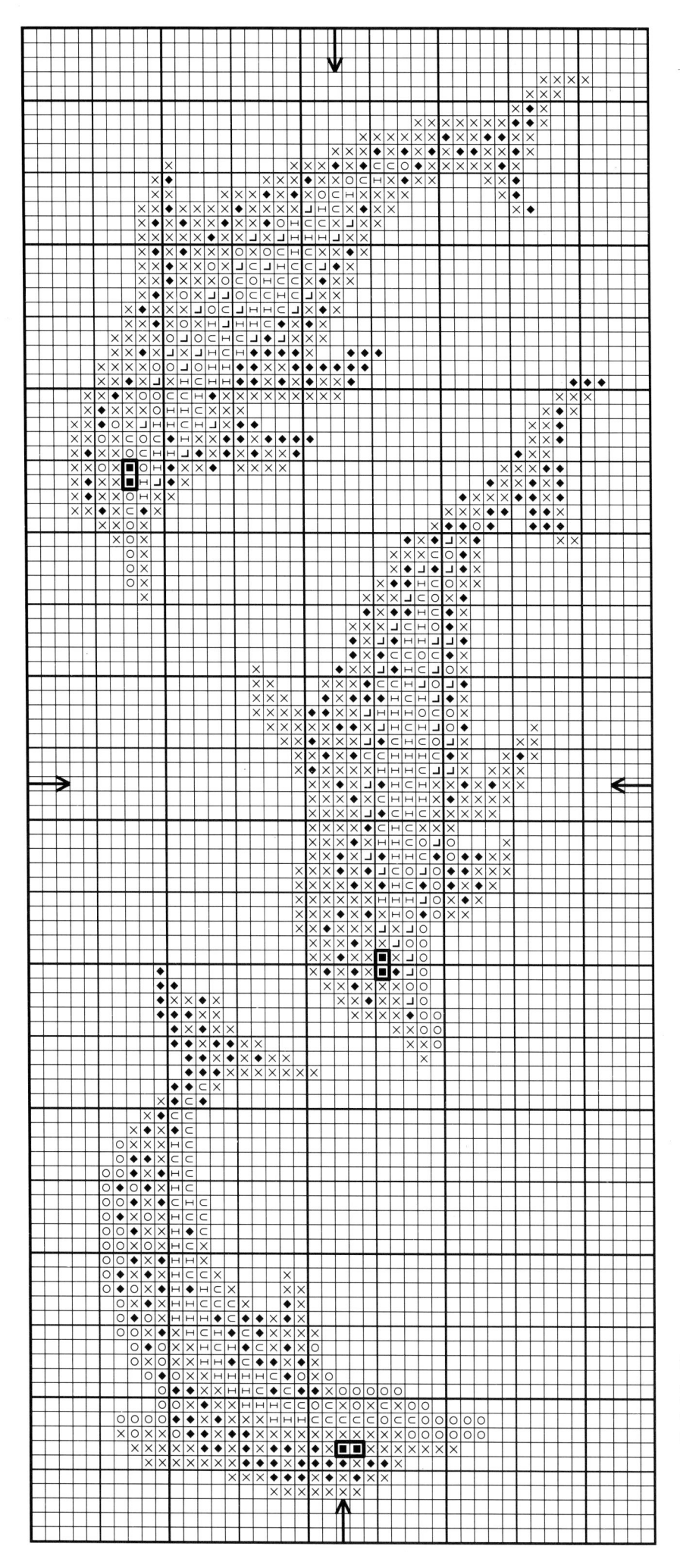

Dolphin Key

DMC Stranded Cotton

- ■ 310 Black
- X 3799 Charcoal
- O 647 Grey
- ◆ 924 Dark Green
- ⌐ 3768 Medium Green
- C 927 Light Green
- I 3072 Silver Grey

DESIGN PORTFOLIO

97

Splendid blue wrens worked in two strands of stranded cotton over two threads of Belfast linen

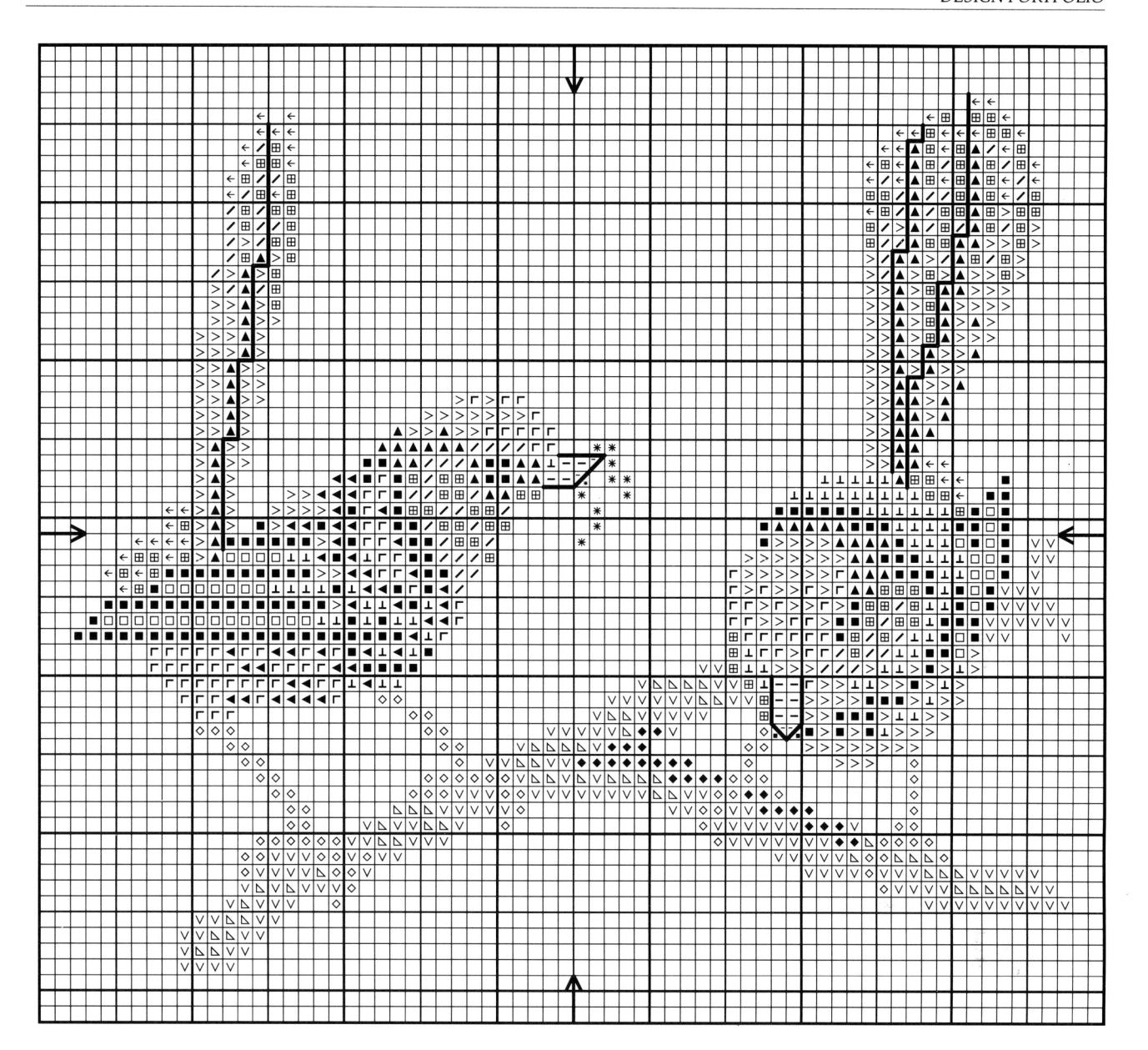

Splendid Blue Wren Key

DMC Threads

- ⌐ 3766 Aqua
- ▫ 561 & 3765 1 Strand of each
- ✳ 834 Camel
- ╱ 518 Ocean Blue
- ← 3761 Pale Aqua
- ⊥ 3765 Peacock Blue
- > 995 Electric Blue
- ◄ 3760 Dull Blue
- ⊞ 996 Turquoise
- ■ 310 Black
- ▲ 930 Dark Greyish Blue
- ◆ 839 Mid Brown
- ◇ 317 Grey
- V 838 Dark Brown
- ◣ 840 Light Brown
- − 844 Charcoal
- ⌐ 310 Outline Beaks & Tails

SOURCEBOOK FOR AUSTRALIAN CROSS-STITCH

Both the mottlecah and the lemon flowering gum designs are worked in three strands of stranded cotton on backgrounds of 14 HPI Aida cloth. The straight stitch flowers and the French knots for the pollen are worked in two strands. Leaf outlines are in one strand. The graph for the lemon flowering gum appears on page 102

DESIGN PORTFOLIO

Mottlecah Key

DMC Stranded Cotton

- ◢ 502 Dark Green
- ⊙ 927 Grey-green
- ⊠ 642 Brown
- Ⓜ 816 Maroon
- Ⓢ 3705 Coral
- • 928 Light Grey-green
- ● 726 Yellow French knots
- ⋀ 3705 Coral straight stitches
- ⌐ 500 Bottle Green back-stitched leaf outllines

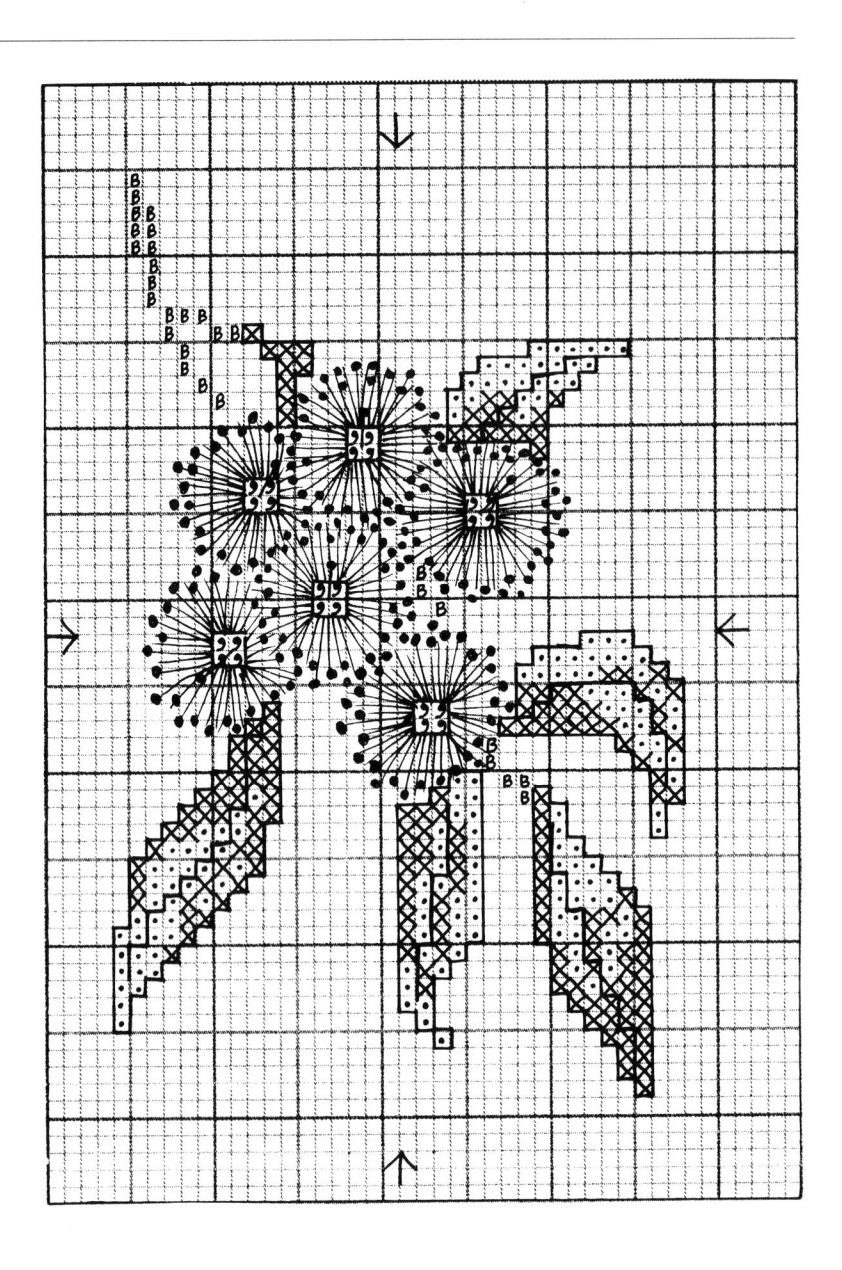

Lemon Flowering Gum Key

DMC Stranded Cotton

- B 3772 Brown
- X 3051 Dark Green
- · 368 Light Green
- 9 772 Pale Lime Green
- ⌐ 919 Dark Rust leaf veins
- ∧∧ 742 Golden Yellow flowers
- • 727 French knots
- ⌐ 500 Bottle Green leaf & flower centre outlines

DESIGN PORTFOLIO

The rosella design is repeated along a strip of Aida band using two strands of stranded cotton

Eastern Rosella Key

DMC Threads

H	937	Dark Green
■	310	Black
⊓	322	Blue
%	740	Orange
●	890	Bottle Green
–	829	Brown
<	726	Yellow
□	907	Lime
O	318	Grey
↑	666	Red
▲	Blanc	White
⌐	666	Outline Throat

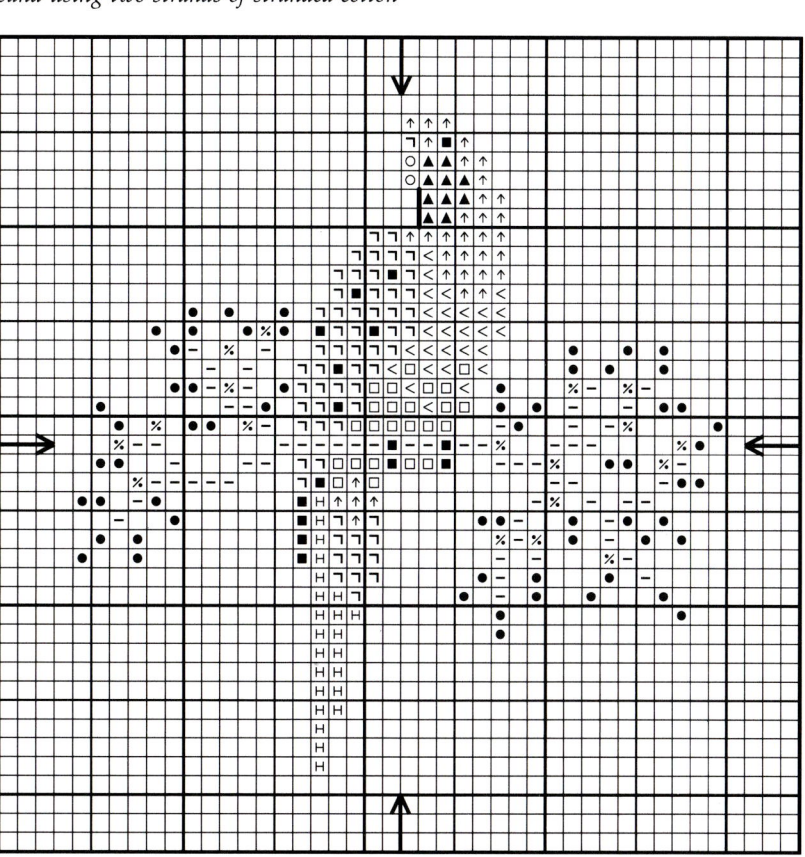

103

Graphs for native orchids on page 46

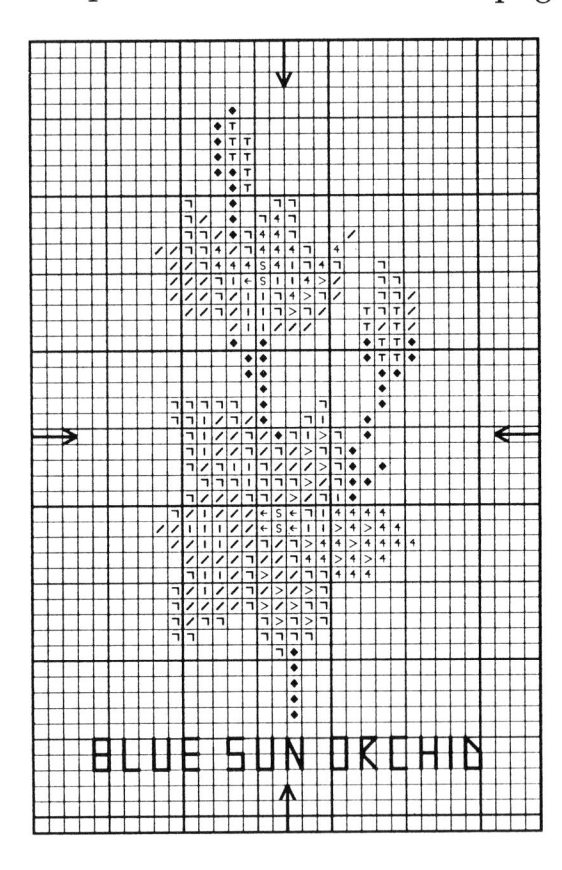

Blue Sun Key

DMC Flower Threads

- ◆ 2730 Dark Green
- T 2732 Light Green
- ⊐ 2325 Light Blue
- ╱ 2826 Mid Blue
- 4 2827 Sky Blue
- ← Blanc White
- I 2825 Dark Blue
- S 2742 Yellow
- > 2337 Very Dark Blue
- ⌐ 2371 Lettering Brown

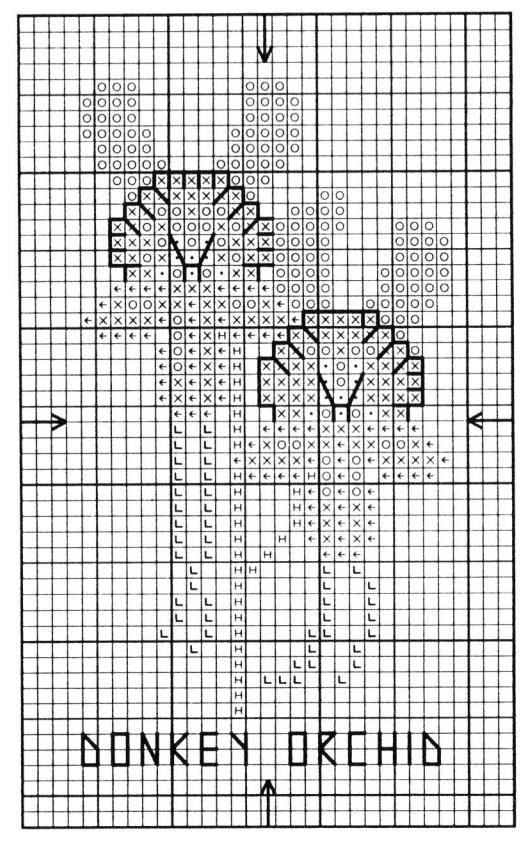

Donkey Orchid Key

DMC Flower Threads

- O 2725 Golden Yellow
- X 2766 Tan
- ← 2354 Rust
- · 2726 Pale Yellow
- L 2907 Light Green
- H 2937 Dark Green
- ⌐ 2371 Lettering Brown
- ⌐ 2354 Rust

DESIGN PORTFOLIO

Graph for bauera daisies border on page 53

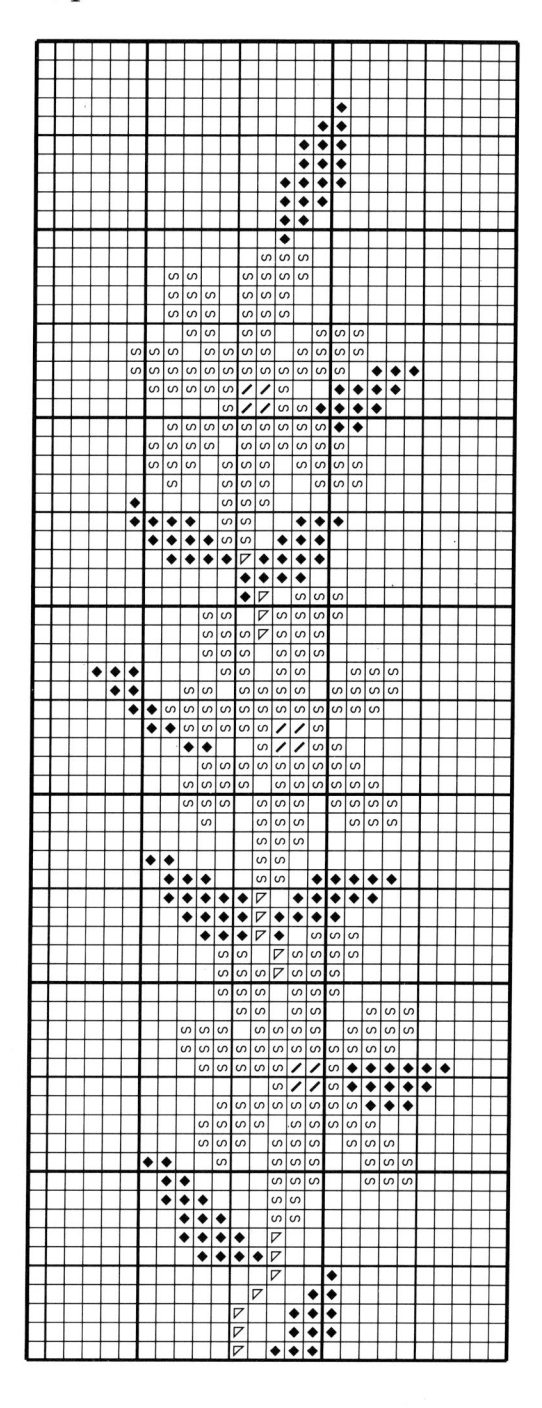

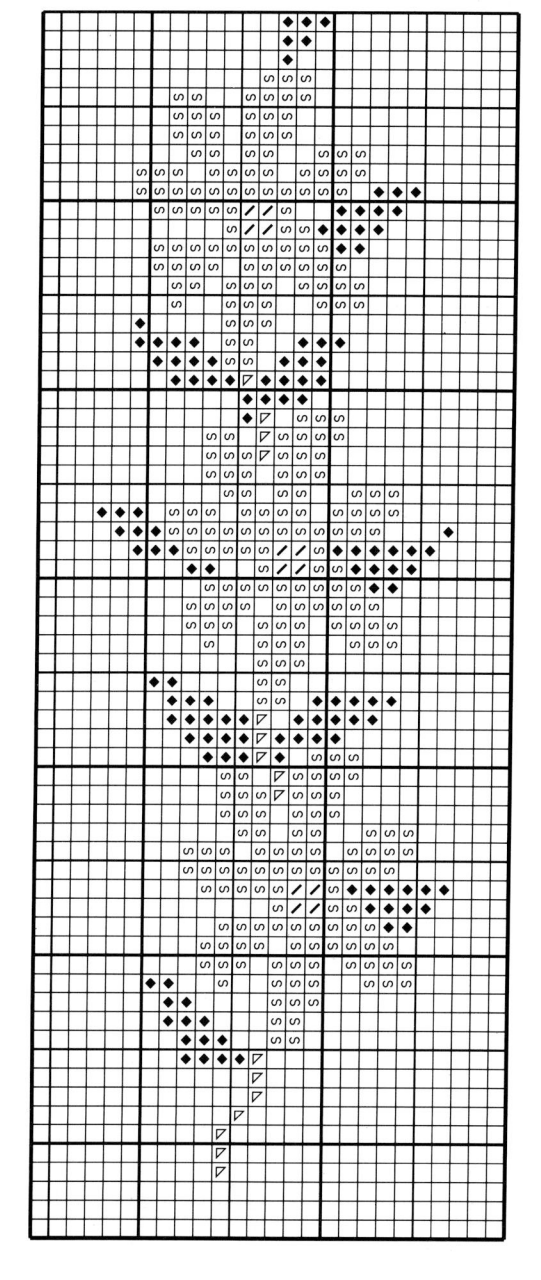

Bauera Daisy Border Key

DMC Variegated Threads

- [S] 62 Pink
- [\] 104 Yellow
- [♦] 122 Green
- [△] 61 Rust

105

Graph for dragonfly on page 57

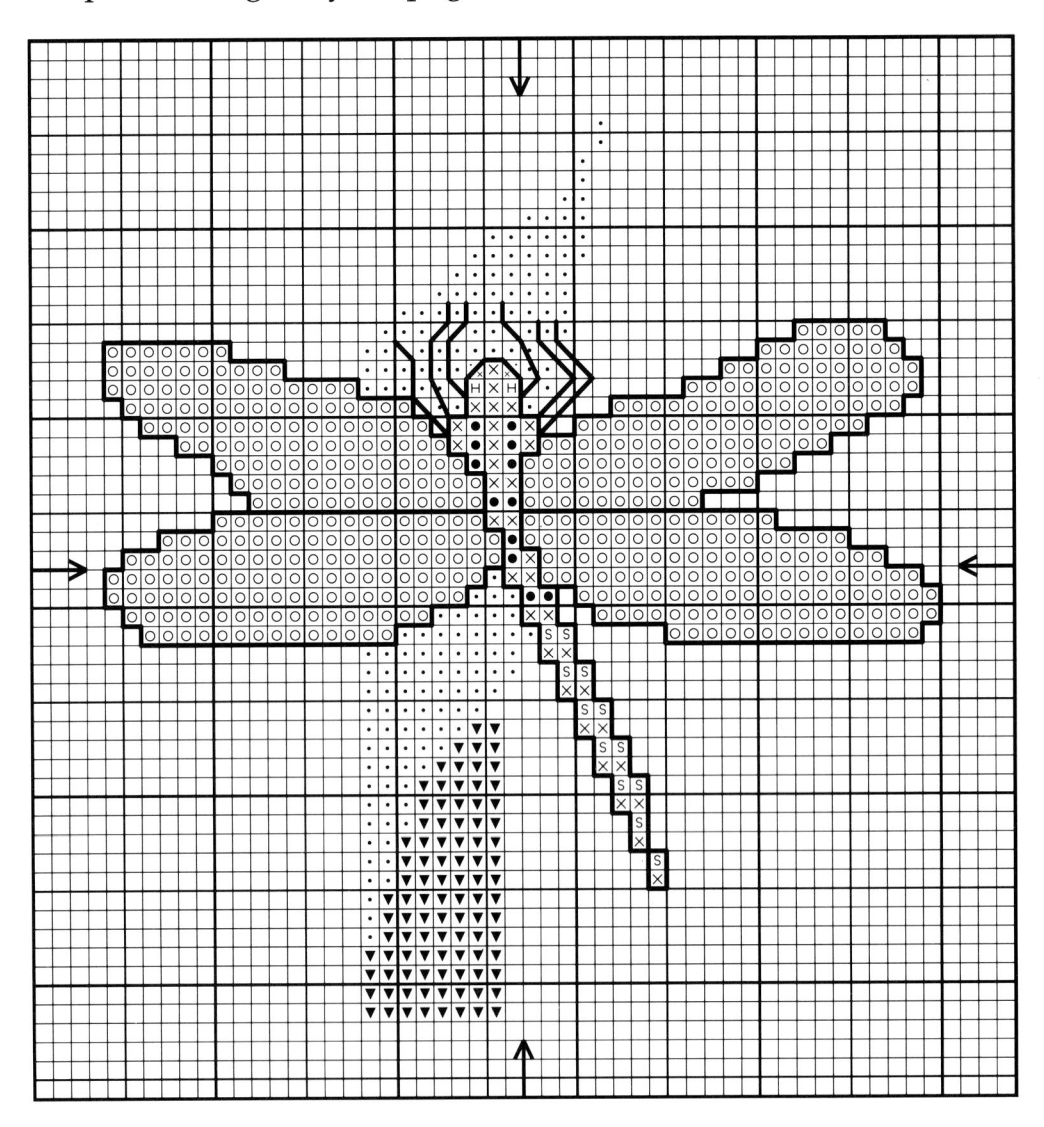

Dragonfly Key

DMC Stranded Cotton

- ⋅ 470 Light Green
- ✗ 869 Brown
- H 995 Electric Blue
- ● 832 Honey
- S 3046 Beige
- ▼ 937 Dark Green
- ⌐ 310 Black Outline

Coats Metallic Thread

- O Pearl

Graph for echidna on page 77

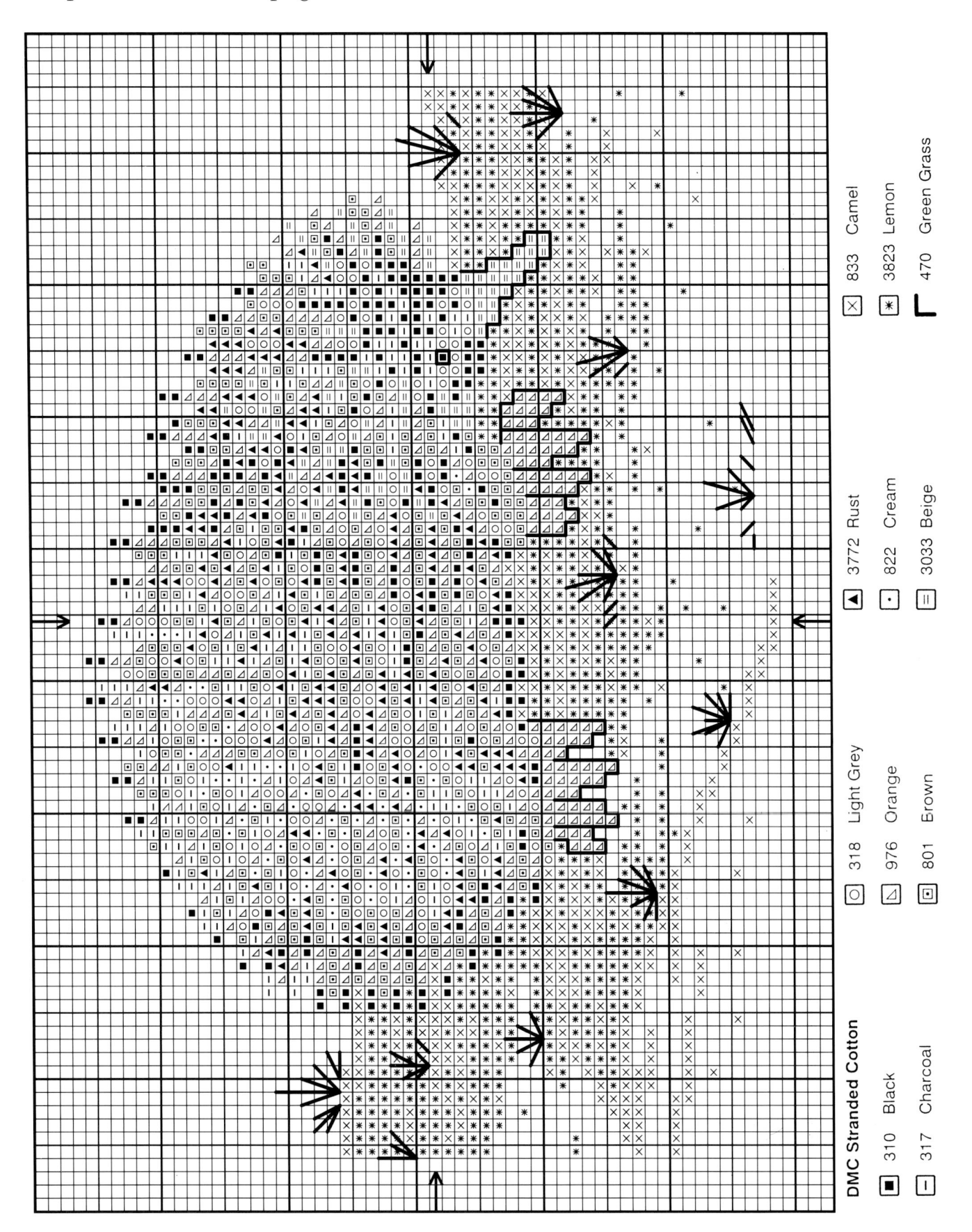

DMC Stranded Cotton

■	310	Black	☒	833	Camel
−	317	Charcoal	✱	3823	Lemon
○	318	Light Grey		470	Green Grass
△	976	Orange	◀	3772	Rust
⊡	801	Brown	·	822	Cream
			‖	3033	Beige

107

Templates for sewing set on page 50

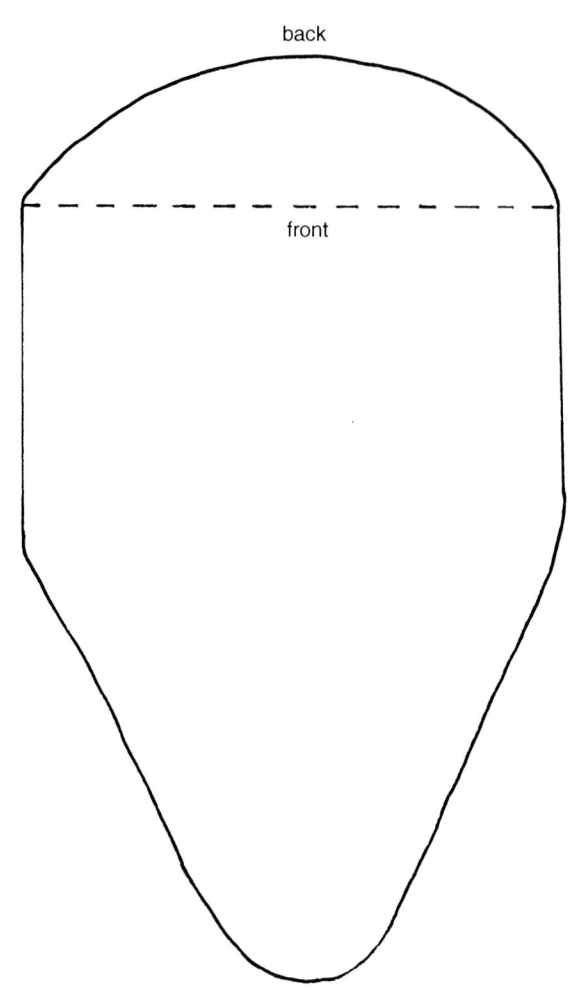

back

front

Card template for scissors case; add 15 mm (5/8") seam allowance

cut 2—front and back

cut pincushion 10 cm x 10 cm (4" x 4")

Card template for needlecase; add 15 mm (5/8") seam allowance

SUPPLIERS

Minnamurra Threads
PO Box 374
Glebe NSW 2037
Mobile 015 403 137

DMC/Myart Needlecraft
51–55 Carrington Road
Marrickville NSW 2204
(02) 9559 3088
For details of your nearest DMC stockist

Porcelain & Lace
Farrell Road
Midvale WA 6056
(09) 250 2502
For hand-painted porcelain pincushion dolls, large $18, small $15 (includes p&p)

The Creative Needle
817a Beaufort St
Inglewood WA 6052
(09) 370 5574

Arts and Crafts Corner
34 Mint Street
Victoria Park WA 6101
(09) 361 4567

Stadia Handcrafts
85 Elizabeth Street
PO Box 495
Paddington NSW 2021
(02) 9328 7900
For details of your nearest stockist of Mill Hill glass beads

Ireland Needlecraft
PO Box 1175
Narre Warren Vic 3805
(03) 9702 3222
For details of your nearest stockist of Kreinik Metallic threads

Rajmahal
Fosterville Road
Bagshot East Vic 3551
(054) 48 8551
For details of your nearest art/silk thread stockist
Mail order available

Hand Made Happiness
201 Hume Highway
Greenacre NSW 2190
(02) 9790 7854
For folk art paints and textile medium

The Crescent Craft Mart
13 The Crescent
Midland WA 6056
(09) 274 3221
For folk art paints, DMC products and glass beads

Tapestry Craft
32 York Street
Sydney NSW 2000
(02) 9299 8588
For full range of craft supplies and threads

Primarily Patchwork
4 Theatre Place
Canterbury Vic 3126
(03) 9830 4537
Printed patchwork fabrics
Mail order and retail

Lavender & Lace
Shop 1, 350 Galston Road
Galston NSW 2159
(02) 9653 1323
For patchwork fabric and folk art paints

Greetings cards available from:
V. Garforth
22 Waterhall Road
South Guildford WA 6055
(09) 2279 6392
$7.50 (inc. postage & packing) for 5 cards

INDEX

Aida band, 26
Aida cloth, 8
Backstitch, 15
Embroidery hoops, 10
Fabric paints, 28
Folk art paints, 28
French knots, 16
Graphs, 12
Kreinik metallics, 23
Monograms, 26
Linen, 8
Metallic braids, 24
Needles, 9
Overdyed threads, 22
Punchwork, 18
Removing dye colour, 19
Silhouettes, 28
Slate frame, 11
Straight stitch, 16
Threads, 10
Thread and fabric guide, 31
Water-soluble pencils, 28